The Certain Way

The Certain Way

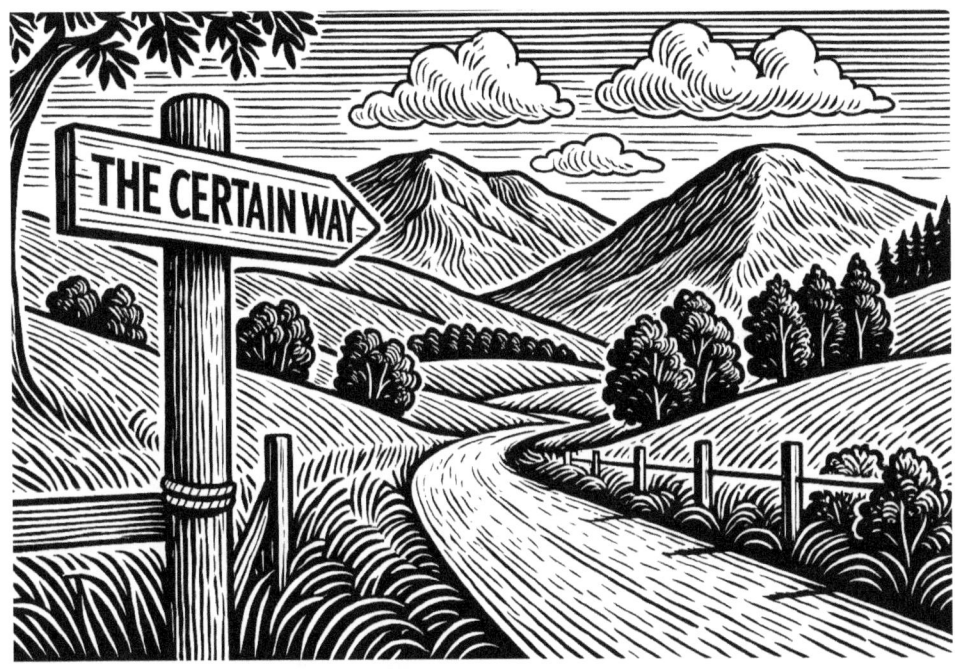

Shoo Rayner

Based on Wallace D. Wattles' classic book
The Science of Getting Rich

THE SCIENCE OF GETTING RICH

BY WALLACE D. WATTLES

The Science of Getting Rich was published in 1910, just a year before Wallace D. Wattles died.

The book became a founding idea behind many of today's self-development and prosperity teachings.

There are very simple, practical ideas at the heart of Wattles' work.

"Always give more in use value than you receive in payment."

And the Golden Rule,

"Do to others as you'd have them do to you."

The world has changed a lot since the book came out and science has moved in directions that Wattles seems to have sensed. When he talks of science in the title of the book, he means to use a formula to be certain of an outcome. So, today, he might say,

"If you practice and apply this formula, you will get rich!"

The purpose of this book is to help you make money, not for money's sake, but because money is the tool that lets you buy the things you need, to create the freedom you desire and to live the life you envision.

Being rich is about more than numbers in a bank account – it's about having the resources to support your dreams, whether that means a home, education for you or your children, coaching, equipment, time to create, or the ability to travel.

Money is how we exchange value in the world today. By learning to act in the Certain Way, you can bring both wealth and richness into your life – the means to fulfil your greatest potential.

> *"The greatest service you can offer to humanity and the Universe is to develop your unique talents and resources to their fullest."*
>
> Wallace D. Wattles

Words & Illustrations Copyright © 2025 Shoo Rayner

All rights reserved.

No part of this publication may be reproduced, stored in a retrieval system, or transmitted in any form or by any means – electronic, mechanical, photocopying, recording, or otherwise – without the prior written permission of the author, except for brief quotations used in critical articles, reviews, or academic discussion.

This book is a reimagining of The Science of Getting Rich by Wallace D. Wattles (originally published in 1910), whose foundational ideas and structure remain at its core. Deep credit and gratitude are due to Wattles for his original work. This modern interpretation is by Shoo Rayner and is based on the lived experience of both authors, past and present.

The thoughts, advice, and interpretations shared here are not financial advice. They are offered in good faith, as reflections and practices that have proved helpful in the authors' own lives.

This is not a sacred text or a blueprint for perfection. It is a conversation, not a commandment – and must not be taken as a rigid doctrine. The author accepts no responsibility for any misinterpretation, misuse, or magical thinking projected onto these pages.

For permissions, enquiries, or correspondence, please visit · fallowground.uk

First edition, 2025

ISBN · 9781908944498

Published by Shoo Rayner

The Certain Way
Table of Contents

	-	PREFACE – 9
CHAPTER 1	-	The Right To Be Rich – 11
CHAPTER 2	-	There Is A Science of Getting Rich – 14
CHAPTER 3	-	Is Opportunity Monopolized? – 18
CHAPTER 4	-	Thought and the Formless Stuff – 22
CHAPTER 5	-	Increasing Life – 25
CHAPTER 6	-	How Riches Come to You – 30
CHAPTER 7	-	Gratitude – 35
CHAPTER 8	-	Thinking in the Certain Way – 39
CHAPTER 9	-	How to Use the Will 43
CHAPTER 10	-	Further Use of the Will – 46
CHAPTER 11	-	Acting in the Certain Way – 49
CHAPTER 12	-	Efficient Action – 54
CHAPTER 13	-	Getting Into The Right Work For You – 59
CHAPTER 14	-	The Impression of Increase – 63
CHAPTER 15	-	The Emerging Self – 67
CHAPTER 16	-	Some Cautions, and Concluding Observations – 70
CHAPTER 17	-	Summary of The Certain Way – 76
	-	POSTSCRIPT – 78
	-	GLOSSARY – 82

PREFACE

This is a practical manual for those whose most pressing need is money, for those who want to get rich first and philosophise later.

It begins with money because, for many, that's the immediate crisis. But this is not a scheme. It's a way of seeing, thinking, and acting that reshapes not just your income, but your life.

It's written for those who don't have the time – or desire – to study philosophy or psychology, but who want results, and are willing to work with what has been repeatedly shown to work – even if the full explanation is still emerging.

You're not expected to question every fundamental idea. Just as you accept gravity without reading Newton, or time without reading Einstein, this book asks you to accept certain working principles and apply them directly.

The principle is simple – follow the method with consistency and focus, and you will get results. Like a scientific formula – do it right, and it works. In this book, science means something practical – a method of observation, thought, and action that leads to consistent outcomes.

This book is a re-writing of The Science of Getting Rich by Wallace Wattles. Wattles grounded his thinking in what he saw as the underlying structure of the Universe.

He published it in 1911 – a moment of radical scientific discovery, between Einstein's theories of relativity and on the cusp of quantum physics.

Wattles wrote plainly and directly for his time. In this re-imagining of Wattles' work, I've worked hard to honour that simplicity and clarity, making it accessible to modern readers without losing its power.

The plan Wattles outlined has helped many. But its success depends entirely on one thing – your willingness to do the work with focus and certainty.

I've included marginal notes drawn from my own repeated readings and lived experience, and have left space for you to make your own. This isn't just a book to read. It's a book to work with.

Chapter One
The Right To Be Rich

Whatever we can say in praise of poverty, the fact remains that it's not possible to live a really complete or successful life unless you have money. You can't fully develop your skills or reach your potential if you're constantly struggling to meet basic needs.

To reveal and develop our inner selves and talents, we need many things and cannot have these things without the money to buy them.

We grow as creative beings – in mind, body, and inner self– by making use of things. The world is structured so that access to those things requires money. If we want to grow, contribute, and live fully, we need a clear, reliable method for building wealth.

The object of all life is growth and development. Everything that lives has an inalienable right to all the growth and development it's capable of. Our right to life includes free, unrestricted access to everything necessary to fully develop our mental, spiritual, and physical lives.

Why the Inner Self Matters

It's easy to focus on the outer game – skills, results, reputation. But without developing your inner self, none of it holds together.

The inner self is your sense of direction, values, and creative drive. It's where clarity, resilience, and originality come from.

When that part of you is weak or neglected, you can get rich and still feel lost. You can be productive and still feel hollow.

Growth isn't just about what you do, it's about who you're becoming underneath.

Real success builds outward from a strong inner core.

What Money Really Buys

Being rich isn't just about having money to spend. It's about time and peace of mind.

Money buys books, courses, tools, and access to experiences that help you grow. It gives you space to reflect, learn, and become who you're meant to be.

Wealth is not the goal – it's the ground from which your best self can grow.

For you, your family, your friends, your work, your world.

In other words, we have a right to be rich.

To be really rich does not mean being satisfied or content with a little. No one should be satisfied with a little if they are capable of using and enjoying more. The purpose of Nature is the advancement and unfolding of life, so everyone should have all they need so they can contribute to the power, elegance, beauty, and richness of life – to be happy with less is a waste.

A person who has all they need to live the life they're capable of is rich. Anyone with plenty of money can have all that they want or need. Life has advanced so far, and become so complex, that even the most ordinary person requires a great amount of wealth in order to live in a manner that even approaches completeness.

Every person naturally wants to become all that they are capable of. This desire to realise innate possibilities is inherent in human nature. We cannot help wanting to be all that we can be.

Success in life is becoming what you want to be.

You can become who you want to be only by engaging with the world around you, and that often requires access to tools, space, and support. Money can bring those things as well as opening doors to shared resources, relationships, and opportunities. So it is essential to understand how wealth is created – not just for spending, but for access, freedom, and growth.

There is nothing wrong in wanting to get rich. The desire for riches is really the desire for a richer, fuller, and more abundant life, and that desire is good. The person who doesn't want to live more abundantly, who doesn't want money enough to buy all they want or need is unusual.

There are three motives for which we live. We live for the body, the mind, and the inner self, neither of which is better or more profound than the other. None of the three can live fully if either of the others is cut short of full life and expression. It's not right or noble to live only for the soul and deny mind or body, and it's wrong to live for the intellect and deny body or inner self.

We've all seen the emptiness that comes from focusing solely on the body while neglecting mind and creative self-expression, and we know that real life means the complete expression of all that we can achieve through body, mind, and the inner self. Whatever anyone says, no one can be really happy or satisfied unless their body is living fully in every function, and unless the same is true of their mind and inner self.

Wherever there is unrealised potential, or a purpose not carried out, there is unsatisfied desire. Desire is potential seeking expression and purpose looking for action.

We cannot live fully in body without good food, comfortable clothing, and warm shelter, nor without freedom from overworking. Rest and recreation are also necessary for physical life.

We cannot live fully in mind without books, education, and time to study, without opportunity for travel and observation, or without intellectual companionship.

Living fully in mind also means engaging in intellectual recreations and surrounding ourselves with the art and beauty we're capable of appreciating.

To live fully as creative beings, we must have love, and love is denied expression by poverty. Our greatest happiness is found in sharing prosperity with those we love. Love expresses itself most naturally and spontaneously through giving.

The person who has nothing to give cannot fill their place as a partner or parent, as a citizen, or as a human being. It's by using material things that we maintain our bodies, develop our minds, and unfold our inner selves. So it is of supreme importance that we should be rich.

As a human being, you cannot help but desire to be rich and it's right that you should do so. It's right and worthwhile to devote your full attention to understanding how to create wealth. It's the noblest and most necessary of all studies. If you neglect this study, you are failing to live up to your full potential.

The Joy of Giving

Our greatest happiness comes from sharing what we have with the people we love.

Love expresses itself most naturally through giving – freely, joyfully, without keeping score.

But if you have nothing to give, you're held back. Poverty helps no one.

We're not just physical beings. We each have an inner self – a spark of awareness, creativity, and connection that wants to grow, express, and contribute.

That drive has been recognised across every culture.

To live fully, that part of you needs room to breathe – and something to give.

What It Really Means to Be Rich

You don't need to be a billionaire or an oligarch to be rich.

In fact, many of those people are poor in spirit – trapped by status, surrounded by hangers-on, and living in fear of loss.

Being rich means having the means to do what you're here to do. And that will look different for everyone.

Chapter Two
There is a Science of Getting Rich

The greatest service you can offer to humanity, the universe and Nature, is to develop your unique abilities and resources to their fullest.

There is a science to getting rich. It's as precise as algebra or arithmetic. Certain laws govern the process of acquiring wealth. When you learn and follow these laws, you can get rich with mathematical certainty.

Wealth comes to those who act in a certain way. Whether by accident or intention, those who follow this way succeed, while those who don't, even if talented or hard-working, often remain poor.

The certain way isn't a secret or a trick – it's a method rooted in consistent, purposeful actions that align with universal laws of success.

It's a natural law that following a formula always produces the same results. Therefore, anyone who learns to do things in a certain way will get rich.

Getting rich is not a matter of environment. If it were, all the people in certain neighbourhoods would become wealthy. The people of one town would all be rich, while those of another would all be poor. The inhabitants of one region would be rolling in money, while those of another would be in poverty.

But wherever you look, you'll see rich and poor living side by side, in the same locality, and often engaged in the same line of work.

When two people live close by and are in the same line of work, and one gets rich while the other remains poor, it shows that getting rich is not primarily a matter of environment.

Some places may be more favourable than others, but when two people in the same line of work are in the same neighbourhood, and one gets rich while the other fails, it suggests that getting rich is the result of doing things in a certain way – following The Certain Way.

What's more, the ability to do things in this Certain Way is not only down to the possession of talent. Many people who have great talent remain poor, while others who have very little talent get rich.

When you study wealthy people, you'll often find they're quite ordinary. They don't get rich because of rare talents or special abilities, but because they do things in a Certain Way.

Getting rich is not the result of saving, or thrift. Many tight-fisted people are poor, while free-spenders often get rich.

Nor is getting rich due to doing things which others fail to do. Two people in the same line of work often do almost exactly the same things, and one gets rich while the other remains poor or fails. All this shows that getting rich comes from doing things in a Certain Way.

What "Certain" Really Means

The word certain can sound mysterious – like secret knowledge you have to discover.

But here, it means something else - sure, reliable, repeatable.

Something you can count on.

Think of it like a recipe. If you follow it properly, you don't need to hope – you can be certain of the result.

Go Where the Energy Is

Some places simply won't support the kind of wealth or work you're here to build.

People have crossed oceans, borders, and brutal terrain in search of opportunity. Sometimes the most powerful move you can make is to relocate – to put yourself where things are happening.

If you're serious about living a wealthy life, you may need to go where the energy is.

Don't let inertia, guilt, or fear of judgment hold you in place.

If getting rich is the result of doing things in a Certain Way, and if following a formula always produces the same results, then anyone who can do things in the same way can become rich. That's when getting rich becomes a matter of science.

Now, is this Certain Way so difficult that only a few can follow it? Not as far as natural ability is concerned – talented people get rich and blockheads get rich – intellectually brilliant people get rich and very stupid people get rich – physically strong people get rich and weak and sickly people get rich.

The ability to think and understand is essential, but anyone who can read and grasp the ideas in this book has what it takes to get rich.

While wealth isn't determined by environment, location does play a role. For instance, few would expect to prosper in the middle of a desert or at the North Pole.

Getting rich means dealing with people. You need to be where people are willing to work with you. If those people are inclined to work in the way you want to work, so much the better. But that is about as far as environment goes. If anyone in your area can get rich, so can you.

Again, it's not a matter of choosing some particular business or profession. People get rich in every business and in every profession, while their next door neighbours, who do the same, remain poor.

It's true that you'll do best working at something you like and which is suited to you. If you have particular talents, you will do best doing something that calls for those talents. You will also do best doing something that is suited to your locality – an ice-cream parlour will do better in a warm climate than in the Arctic, and a luxury car dealership will likely fail in a low-income area. A bakery would thrive in a busy neighbourhood but struggle in a remote, industrial area with no passing trade.

Getting rich does not depend upon your working in some particular business or profession, but upon your learning to do things in a Certain Way. If you are now in a line of work, and anyone else in your locality is getting rich doing the same thing while you are not getting rich, it's because you are not doing things in the same way that they are.

You don't need money to start – you need direction.

Having money can make things easier. But this isn't about what you already have – it's about how you begin. Many who are now wealthy started with nothing but a clear intention and consistent action.

If you start working in the Certain Way, money and resources will begin to show up. That's not wishful thinking – it's part of the process.

No matter your starting point – whether you're deeply in debt, without friends or resources – you can begin building wealth by acting in the Certain Way. Success isn't about where you start – it's about the formula you follow.

Take Action

Don't wait. Today is the best time to begin. Make a decision. Take the first step. Write down what you'll do tomorrow.

The easiest thing in the world is to keep putting off today until tomorrow.

Set Sail on the Tide

William Shakespeare wrote:

"There is a tide in the affairs of men which, taken at the flood, leads on to fortune... We must take the current when it serves, or lose our ventures."

He understood something vital – timing matters.

If you don't seize your moment, it passes. And once it's gone, it may not return.

None of this is new. Shakespeare knew it – and he learned it from the thinkers who came before him.

Certainty means acting when the tide is flowing.

Chapter Three
Is Opportunity Monopolised?

The best time to start is now, no matter your past or circumstances.

The Certain Way to get rich begins here.

No one is kept poor because others have fenced off all the opportunities or monopolised all the wealth. Some types of work may seem out of reach, but new opportunities are always emerging.

It would be difficult to become the owner of Google or Instagram today, as these businesses are well-established. But artificial intelligence is still in its infancy, offering exciting opportunities – whether by building AI-driven solutions, applying AI to existing businesses, or creating entirely new industries with it.

If you are an employee of a huge corporation, you have little chance of becoming the CEO. But, if you start acting in a Certain Way, you can soon leave your current job for a better one that might lead to the top – or even to starting your own business.

These days, thanks to the internet, the barriers to entry for entrepreneurs are lower than ever. Platforms like Etsy and Payhip make it easy to set up shop in very little time, while social media lets you promote your products and services directly to customers. Dipping your toe into entrepreneurship – perhaps by starting a side hustle – lets you test your ideas with minimal risk while building your confidence and skills.

At different moments in time, opportunities can shift with people's changing needs and the tides of cultural transformation.

Currently, the tide is moving towards new areas like AI, robotics, renewable energy, space exploration and, back on Earth, elder care genetics, medicine and environmental concerns. Today, opportunity is wide open to all with little required upfront. There are opportunities for creators to reach their fans and audiences directly and, for businesses with products to promote, to reach customers through online influencers.

There is so much opportunity if you will go with the tide, instead of trying to swim against it. You are not deprived of opportunity, nor are you trapped by the system. Your current circumstances are shaped by the way you've done things up until now. But the moment you begin to act in the Certain Way, everything can change.

When you begin to do things in the Certain Way, you begin to succeed and grow rich. The principles of wealth are the same for you as they are for all others.

Learn this, or choose to remain where you are. As long as you carry on doing the same thing day after day you will not move forward. You are not held back by ignorance or your position in society. You can follow the tide of opportunity to riches, and this book will tell you how.

No one is kept in poverty by a lack in the supply of riches – there is more than enough for all. The visible supply is practically inexhaustible, and the invisible supply really is inexhaustible. Everything you see on earth is made from one Original Substance – the Formless Stuff from which all things are made.

We Keep Creating

Humans are extraordinary. When one resource runs out, we find another – often a better one.

Who might have imagined, in the age of oil, that data would become the most valuable resource of the next century?

Data is intangible. It moves through chips, cables – even the air. You can't touch it, but it fuels the modern world.

Humans are wired to adapt, invent, and keep going.

New opportunities will always emerge as people seek solutions, connection, and a better way to live.

The Myth of Scarcity

The belief in scarcity is one of the biggest blocks to understanding how the world really works, and to building a rich, meaningful life.

Nature is open, abundant, and available to you.

You are a temporary steward of that abundance, a participant in its flow.

What you do with it is up to you.

You can gorge and you can hoard, but that path leads away from meaning.

Wealth isn't about what you take. It's about how you grow, share, and create.

New things are constantly created as older things decay or are recycled – but everything, seen and unseen, comes from the same source - the limitless supply of the Formless Stuff.

The universe is made from it, but not all of it was used up. The spaces in, through, and between the shapes and forms of the visible universe are permeated and filled with the Formless Stuff – which is the raw material of everything.

When visible supplies run low, humanity innovates – developing new technologies, discovering alternative materials, and finding creative ways to recycle what we already have. Much more than has ever been made can still be made, and even then we won't run out of the supply of the universal raw material – the Formless Stuff. So no one is poor because Nature is poor, or because there is not enough to go around.

When the supply of building material is exhausted, new materials will be devised. Nature is an inexhaustible store of riches, the supply will never run short. The Formless Stuff is alive with creative energy, and is constantly producing new things. Throughout history, when resources have dried up, humanity has discovered innovative ways to replenish or replace them, often inspired by nature's own cycles of renewal.

When oil runs out, humanity will harness the sun, wind, and fusion to meet its energy needs. If all the gold and silver on Earth runs out, and if we still need them, we will find new ways to extract it – perhaps even from asteroids, which are rich in precious materials that and waiting to be exploited.

The Formless Stuff responds to the needs of mankind, and won't let us be without the things we require. This is true of mankind collectively which, as a whole, is always abundantly rich. If individuals are poor, it's because they don't follow the Certain Way of doing things which makes individuals rich.

The Formless Stuff is intelligent stuff that thinks. It's alive and brimming with a natural urge to grow, create, and realise its potential. It's the way of intelligence to want to grow and of consciousness to extend its boundaries and find fuller expression. The universe of forms has been made by Formless Living Stuff, turning itself into shapes and things in order to express itself more fully.

Nature is the great living presence, always moving toward more life and fuller expression. It's deepest urge is for growth, and its driving force is the increase of life in all forms.

Everything that can contribute to that increase is already provided for, in abundance. There is no lack – unless Nature, infinite and self-consistent, were to contradict itself.

But it does not.

Wattles runs two lines of thought in parallel throughout this chapter – and through his book.

The first is statistical and practical – what we'd now call following the data. He advises us to look for what works, what sells, where the activity is. This is pragmatic advice – go where the demand already exists and offer something of value. It's about probability – positioning yourself where success is statistically more likely.

The second idea is more foundational and metaphysical and, in many ways, it anticipates quantum theory. Wattles suggests that everything is ultimately made of the same fundamental substance or energy, and that it is Nature – not blind chance – that brings form into being.

But Nature does use chance – variation, randomness, uncertainty – as part of its creative process. It's not mechanical, but it's not arbitrary either.

We are co-creators with Nature, able to bring new forms into the world through the clarity and consistency of our thought.

What Is Form?

 *The idea of form dates back to Plato and Aristotle.*

Form is the essential structure or defining quality of a thing, distinct from the material it's made of.

Look at your hand.

It's made of flesh and bone. It's built from cells, from molecules, from elements, from atoms, from particles...

...all the way down to what we might call Formless Stuff, the invisible stuff from which all things are made.

None of it is fixed. Every part of you was once something else – food, water, air.

You're built from matter recycled through slime moulds, fungi, plants, and animals – again and again since life began – and all of it powered by the sun.

Form is not static. It is structure in motion – shaped by life, through time.

What is a Field?

In science, a field is something that fills space and carries force.

You can't always see it – but it affects everything in it.

Gravity is a field. Magnetism is a field. Light, sound, even weather. They are all shaped by fields.

Think of a field as an invisible structure, like the wind shaping a sand dune, or a radio signal filling a room. It's there, even if you can't see it.

Now imagine a field that responds to thought – not just matter or motion.

That's what this book means by Nature as a living, intelligent field. It doesn't just hold energy – it responds to intention.

Fields are how invisible forces shape real things.

Chapter Four
Thought and the Formless Stuff

You are not kept poor by a lack in the supply of riches. The boundless resources of Nature are freely open to you. As you continue reading, you'll discover how your thoughts and actions can align with these resources through the Certain Way.

At the root of it all is Thought – the invisible force that brings form out of the formless.

Everything begins with a thought held in Nature, that is a living, intelligent field that responds to intention.

When a clear thought is impressed into this field, the form it imagines begins to take shape.

That's not philosophy – that's just how it is. It's how the oak tree begins, how the planets formed, and how all invention comes into being. Every form and action began first as a thought in the thinking field of Nature, which then moved the Formless Stuff into form.

We live in a thought-world. The universe itself emerged as a thought expanding through the formless field. Nature imagined stars, and stars came to be. Nature imagined oaks, and oaks began to grow. The process is gradual, patterned, and responsive. The thought of a form does not instantly produce the thing, but it sets processes in motion.

Nature – the living system which you are a part of – does not operate by magic, but by intention working through time. Its thoughts follow patterns, like plans unfolding. That's why a tree takes time to grow, or why a house requires architecture, labour, and materials to emerge from a single vision.

Every creation begins with a thought – whether in the mind of Nature or in yours. You were made to think, not just to react. You are a centre of thought, a node in Nature's larger intelligence, capable of original vision and creative will.

So far, humanity has used thought mostly to shape what already exists – rearranging wood and metal, refining materials, adjusting forms. With 3D printing, CRISPR, and AI, we're already creating new forms – not by accident, but through focused thought and clear process.

As thinking beings, we can go beneath the level of materials, to the Formless Stuff itself. By impressing our thoughts into the field of Nature, we begin the formation of things at the most foundational level.

There are three core principles behind this idea:

1. Everything begins in the formless. Nature is a living, intelligent field – the raw potential from which all things emerge.

2. Thought is the catalyst. When a clear thought is placed into this field, the imagined form begins to take shape.

3. We are active participants. As thinking centres, we can impress our intentions into Nature – initiating the creation of what we clearly and consistently imagine.

That's the whole mechanism of riches and creation.

There is no need for mysticism here. This is not magical thinking. It is creative discipline – the ability to think with clarity and certainty, to hold to the truth beneath appearances.

Form Doesn't Appear by Magic

Nothing new appears out of nowhere. We turn thought into form by following real rules and processes, step by step.

But thought alone isn't enough.

We have to act, build, and engage with the process. That's how the new form meets us.

Science helps us understand the deeper principles behind how things work. It gives us new tools, systems, and methods – so we can shape what once seemed impossible.

But every new form still requires effort. New forms show up through action – not just imagination.

Form builds on form. Thought builds on thought.

That's how progress happens.

The Real Work

This chapter is the heart of the book.

In the age of the internet, we're flooded with ideas – some shallow, some manipulative, some just noise. Holding on to what's real – and thinking in terms of growth and abundance – is harder than it looks.

The hardest work in the world is to keep your mind on what's true.

It's easy to become lost to conspiracies, scams, gurus, and rabbit holes. But the Certain Way means not getting pulled off course.

You're not denying suffering or scarcity. You're just refusing to treat them as the whole story, or the final word.

Keep your eye on the goal. That's the work. That's the Certain Way.

Thinking truth – especially when appearances show lack or chaos – is the hardest work in the world. But it's also the most powerful. You begin to shape your life not by reacting to what is, but by focusing on what could be – and then walking that thought into being.

This is the core of the Certain Way. Not hustling. Not wishing. But thinking truth with discipline – and aligning your actions accordingly.

You don't have to believe it blindly, but to work with it, you need to engage with the principle – fully, and without half-measures.

It's not about faith. It's about focus. You're not asked to believe. You're asked to practice.

There is a formless stuff from which all things are made. In its original state, it fills, permeates, and surrounds all things – even the spaces between them.

A thought, held clearly and impressed into this substance, begins to shape itself into form.

Nature is the living intelligence that receives and responds to thought. When we think of and sustain a clear image – with purpose and certainty – we set that image into motion, and the thing we think about begins to take shape.

Dwell on these statements. Let them become your foundational thinking. Not as wishful slogans – but as structural facts.

The moment you understand this, you stop flinching at appearances. You stop reacting. You start building.

This is the beginning of wealth.

Chapter Five
Increasing Life

You must completely let go of the belief that a higher power wants you to be poor or that your poverty serves any divine purpose.

Nature is all and it exists in all. You live within it and Nature lives within you. Being a consciously living force, it has the inherent desire of every living intelligence for the increase of life.

Every living thing must continually aim to expand its life because life, through the mere act of living, must increase itself.

A seed, dropped into the ground, bursts into activity, and in the act of living produces a hundred more seeds. One pomegranate on a tree can have up to a thousand seeds. Life, by living, multiplies itself. Life is always evolving – growth is essential for its continuation.

Intelligence also demands continuous growth. Every thought we think makes us think of another thought – consciousness is continually expanding. Every fact we learn leads us to learn another fact – knowledge is continually increasing.

Read Until It's Yours

Read this book until its ideas become second nature – until you can draw on them instinctively, like a shield against doubt or contradiction.

We live in an age of loud voices and constant influence – and yes, even this book is influencing you.

But influence is a choice.

You can decide what you watch, read, and listen to.

Don't submit to the fire-hose of fear, noise, and negativity that comes from the media, your friends, or even your own habits.

Stay true to your thoughts. That's where your direction begins.

The Real Meaning of Desire

The desire for riches is simply the potential of a larger life trying to come into being.

As you grow and create, your ideas multiply. Your horizons expand. You begin to see what's truly possible.

Riches aren't just physical things. They include the intangible – friendship, love, family, honour – all of which make you rich in a deeper sense.

Nature wants you to be rich – not for wealth itself, but because it expresses more of itself through you when you have the means to act, create, and give.

It's as if the future you've glimpsed – and quietly believed in – is pulling you toward the moment it becomes real.

Every talent we cultivate inspires us to cultivate another. We are compelled by the urge of life seeking fulfilment. It drives us on to know more, to do more, and to be more and, as such, we must have more. We must have things to use, for we learn and do, and become only by using things.

We must get rich, so we can live more. The desire for riches is simply the potential of a larger life trying to exist. Every desire is the effort of an unexpressed possibility wanting to become a reality. It's the possibility of the reality that causes the desire. The desire for more wealth is no different from the natural urge that makes plants grow – it is life seeking greater expression.

Nature is also subject to these principles of life – it's infused with the desire to live more – that is why it can't stop creating things. Nature wants to live more in you and through you, therefore it wants you to have all the things that you can use.

It's the desire of Nature that you should get rich. It wants you to get rich because it can express itself better through you if you have plenty of things to use in giving it expression. It can live more in you if you have unlimited command of the means of life. Nature wants you to have everything you need and want.

Nature is friendly to your plans. Everything is naturally for you. Make up your mind that this is true, but it is essential that your purpose be in harmony with Nature's purpose.

You must want real life, not mere pleasure or sensual gratification. Life is about fulfilling our potential, and we only truly live when we engage fully in our physical, mental, and spiritual capacities – without overdoing any of them.

You don't want to get rich to be self-indulgent, to gratify your base, animal desires – that is not life. Living fully means embracing every aspect of life, including the needs of the body. Ignoring your physical impulses or denying them healthy, natural expression leaves life incomplete.

You don't seek wealth just to enjoy intellectual pursuits, to gain knowledge or to achieve ambition, to outshine others, or to become famous. While these can all be meaningful parts of life, focusing solely on intellectual pleasures leads to an unbalanced existence – and you'll never feel truly fulfilled that way.

You don't want to get rich solely for the good of others, losing yourself in the saving of others, just to experience the joys of philanthropy and sacrifice. Inner joys are only a part of life, and they are no better or nobler than any other.

You want to get rich in order to eat, drink, and be merry, when the time is right. You want to surround yourself with beautiful things, to travel, to feed your mind and develop your intellect, so you can love all, do kind things and play a part in helping the world to find truth.

Remember, extreme altruism is no better or nobler than extreme selfishness – both are misguided. Get rid of the idea that a deity wants you to sacrifice yourself for others so you can secure their favour by doing so – nothing of the sort is required of you.

It's far better that you make the most of yourself, for yourself and for others, and you can help others more by making the most of yourself than in any other way.

On an aircraft, you're instructed to put on your oxygen mask before helping others during an emergency. Without oxygen, you are helpless and of no use to anyone, in fact you become a burden.

Similarly, you can help others by getting rich first, so it's right and admirable that you give your best and primary thoughts to the work of acquiring wealth. Poverty helps no one.

Remember, however, that the desire of Nature is for all, and its actions must be for more life to all. It cannot be made to work for less life to anyone, because Nature is equally in everyone, seeking riches and life for all.

Nature will make things for you, but it will not take things away from someone else and give them to you.

You must get rid of the idea of competition. You must create and not compete for what is already created. You don't have to take anything away from anyone.

You don't have to be a ruthless negotiator, to cheat or take advantage. You don't have to pay anyone less than their work is worth.

You don't have to hanker after other people's property, or view it with envy. No one has anything that you can't also have, and you don't need to take from them what they already have.

What Being Rich Really Means

You'll start to realise that riches, in the Certain Way, aren't about yachts, fast cars, or a life of diamonds and champagne.

Nature wants you to be rich so you can fulfil your potential.

That starts with basics – food, shelter, stability.

If you value beauty, fine food, or even a mansion, that's part of your desire – and that's valid.

But remember – the more you have, the more you have to manage. Every possession comes with responsibility – your time, your energy, or someone else's who you have to pay and manage.

Being rich isn't about the trappings of wealth.

It's about the freedom to do what you're here to do.

Don't Be Distracted by Giants

It's easy to feel frustrated by governments and corporations.

But in their own way – knowingly or not – they're doing Nature's work on a larger scale.

Some changes require massive systems and collective power.

That doesn't mean they matter more. It just means they play a different role.

Eventually, those structures will fade into history.

Your task is not to fix or fight them – but to make the most of your time, your choices, and the opportunity of life you've been given.

Focus here. Focus now.

You are going to be a creator, not a competitor. You are going to get what you want in such a way that when you get it, everyone will have more than they have now.

It's true that there are those who get a vast amount of money by doing the exact opposite of the statements in the paragraph above. These oligarchs and titans of industry sometimes become very rich purely by their extraordinary ability on the field of competition. Sometimes they unconsciously relate themselves to Nature in its great purpose and action for the general growth of mankind through industrial evolution.

Microsoft, Google, facebook, Amazon, Apple, and many, others, have been the unconscious agents of Nature in the necessary work of organizing the digital world we now live in. In the end, their work will have contributed immensely toward increased life for all. They have reorganized the world, but they will soon be succeeded by new disrupters, wielding new technologies, just as they disrupted the old, analogue world that they changed forever.

The billionaires are like the monster reptiles of the prehistoric eras, they play a necessary part in the evolutionary process, but the same power that produced them will see them fade away. And, have they been really rich? Have they lived complete and fulfilling lives?

Riches gained competitively are never satisfactory or permanent. They are yours today, and another's tomorrow. Remember, if you are to become rich in a scientific and certain way, you need to move completely beyond a competitive mindset.

Never believe for a second that wealth is limited. As soon as you begin to think that all the money is being cornered or controlled by bankers and others, and that laws should be passed to stop them, and so on – in that moment you drop into the competitive mindset, and your power to cause creation is gone for the time being, and what is worse, you will probably stop the creative actions you've already set going.

Know that there are countless riches on and in the Earth that have not yet been found or used and that if there weren't, more would be created to supply your needs. The human race is already reaching out to the stars where an infinite supply awaits, while on Earth, new value has be created out of thin air in the digital world.

Trust that the money and things you need will come, even if it requires thousands of people to start new ventures or to make groundbreaking discoveries first, they will come in time and when you are ready.

Never look at the visible supply, always look at the limitless riches in the Formless Stuff, and know that they are coming to you as fast as you can receive and use them. Nobody, is cornering the visible supply, or preventing you from getting what is yours.

So, never allow yourself to think for a moment that all the things you want will be sold before you are able to get them, unless you hurry. Don't ever worry about the corporations or billionaires, or worry that they will soon own the whole earth.

Never be afraid that you'll lose what you want because someone else beats you to it. That cannot possibly happen as you are not seeking anything that is possessed by anyone else. You are causing what you want to be created from Formless Stuff, where the supply is limitless.

Stick to the core principle of the Certain Way:

- **There is a formless stuff from which all things are made. In its original state, it fills, permeates, and surrounds all things – even the spaces between them.**
- **A thought, held clearly and impressed into this substance, begins to shape itself into form.**
- **Nature is the living intelligence that receives and responds to thought. When we think of and sustain a clear image – with purpose and certainty – we set that image into motion, and the thing we think about begins to take shape.**

A Time of Limitless Opportunity

It may feel like we're dominated by giant corporations – but we also have unprecedented access and opportunity through the platforms they run.

We can order almost anything and have it by tomorrow.

We can connect, collaborate, and create with people across the world and find customers, audiences, and friends in ways we never imagined.

All human knowledge – and the tools to access and exploit it – are at our fingertips.

This is an extraordinary time to be alive. Use it well.

The Core Idea - Value Exchange

Always give more in use value than you take in payment. That's the heart of the Certain Way.

It doesn't mean undercharging or working for free.

It means that what you offer, in experience, outcome, or impact, should feel worth more to the person receiving it than the money they gave you.

A good product, a helpful service, a meaningful experience, these things create real value. They solve a problem, meet a need, or make someone's life better.

Money is just one side of the exchange. The value you create is the other.

When you consistently give more in value than you take in payment, you create trust, growth, and momentum for everyone involved.

That's how wealth flows. That's the Certain Way.

Chapter Six
How Riches Come to You

We've established that you don't have to be a ruthless negotiator, to cheat, take advantage or offer shady deals.

That doesn't mean you don't have to offer any deals, or that you are above having to deal with anyone at all.

You don't have to try to get something for nothing or deal with people unfairly. You can give to everyone more than you take from them.

You can't give everyone more in market value than you take from them, but you can give more in use value than you take in payment – that way, every transaction adds to life.

The paper, ink, and other materials in this book may not be worth the money you pay for it, but if the ideas the book gives you bring you riches, you've not been wronged by those who sold it to you – they've given you a great use value for a small monetary value.

Imagine offering a £1,500 luxury holiday to a market trader – right in the middle of their busiest season – in exchange for £500. It sounds generous, but it costs them more than money – time, missed income, lost momentum. It adds stress, not value.

Now imagine instead, you offer a mobile card reader and a solar charger – tools that help them serve more customers and grow their income.

Real value isn't about cost – it's about context and usefulness. That's the principle. Always give more in use value than you take in payment.

When you operate from a creative, and not a competitive mindset, every transaction should leave others better off than before. If you thrive by offering things that people don't truly need or that don't enrich their lives, it's worth re-evaluating your life and transition to a position where you can genuinely create value for others.

Give everyone more in use value than you take from them in monetary value, then you are adding to the life of the world with every transaction you make either as an employee or in your own business.

If you employ people, then you need to take from them more in monetary value than you pay them in wages. But make it so that your business runs on the principle of advancement, so that each employee who wishes, can progress a little every day.

You can make your business do for your employees what this book is doing for you. You can conduct your business so it's like a sort of ladder, so every employee who makes the effort can climb the ladder to riches too. And if they choose not to, that is their own decision.

Here's the key point. Because you are to cause the creation of your riches from Formless Stuff which permeates all your environment, it does not follow that your riches are going to appear out of thin air. They are not going to appear before your eyes in a puff of theatrical smoke!

If you want a laptop, for instance, you can't simply impress the thought of it on Thinking Substance and expect it to appear by magic.

You must hold the mental image of the laptop with complete certainty that it is being made, or that it is already on its way to you.

The Trouble with "Manifestation"

There's a modern idea that you can manifest anything by just "putting it out to the Universe." Say the affirmation. Visualise it hard enough. Wait. Receive.

But this skips the most important part – action.

You don't get what you want by declaring it. You get it by thinking clearly, aligning your actions, and following through – even when it's hard.

Manifestation without action is just fantasy. The Certain Way isn't passive. It's disciplined, intentional, and creative.

Not incantation – but direction, backed by consistent effort.

Create, Don't Compete

We're raised to compete – to run faster, jump higher, earn more. Wanting the best is human. Winning isn't wrong.

But in your work and transactions, aim to be creative rather than competitive – so that both sides gain.

Creativity isn't just art or music that stirs the soul. It's the power to shape ideas into forms that serve, inspire, and bring value to everyone involved.

That's the Certain Way. Everyone wins.

Don't question the process. Never speak of it or think of it in any way other than as something that is sure to arrive.

Claim it as *yours* already. It will be brought to you by the power of Nature acting upon the minds of people. If you live in England, it might be that someone from Sweden or Japan needs to engage in a transaction that results in you eventually getting what you want.

If so, then it will be as much to their advantage as it's to yours.

Don't forget – Nature is in all, through all, and communicates with all. It can influence all.

Nature – the Thinking Substance – desires fuller life and better living. That desire has already created all the laptops, tablets and computers ever made, and that desire can cause the creation of millions more, and will too, whenever someone sets the process in motion by desire and by acting in a Certain Way.

You can certainly have a laptop, and it's just as certain that you can have anything else you can use for the advancement of your own life and the lives of others.

Don't hesitate to ask big – Nature wants to live all that is possible in and through you, and it's Nature's pleasure to give you all you want and need. It wants you to have all that you can or will use for the living of the most abundant life.

If you get clear in your mind the fact that the desire you feel for riches is the same as Nature's desire for fuller expression, your certainty will become unshakable.

Wallace Wattles, who wrote the original version of this book in 1910, described seeing a little boy sitting at a piano. The boy was frustrated by his inability to play real music. When asked why he was so upset, the lad said, "I can feel the music in me, but I can't make my hands go right."

The music in him was the *urge* of Nature containing all the possibilities of life. All of music was seeking expression through the child.

Nature is trying to live, act, and enjoy through humanity. It wants hands to build magnificent structures, to play beautiful music, to create great works of art. It wants eyes to see its beauty, tongues to speak mighty truths, and mouths to sing inspiring songs.

All that there is of possibility is seeking expression through mankind. Nature wants those who can make music to have instruments to play on, and to have the means to cultivate their talents to the fullest extent.

It wants those who can appreciate beauty to be able to surround themselves with beautiful things, and those who can discern truth to have every opportunity to travel and observe. It wants those who appreciate clothes to be beautifully dressed, and those who appreciate good food to be fed like royalty.

Nature wants all these things because it's Nature that enjoys these things through us. The desire you feel for riches is Nature, aiming to express itself in you, as it tried to find expression through the little boy at the piano.

So, don't hesitate to ask for a lot. Your part is to focus and express your desire to Nature.

This is a difficult point with most people. They retain something of the old idea that poverty and self-sacrifice are a good thing. They look on poverty as a part of the plan, a necessity of nature. They have the idea that Nature has finished its work, and that the Universe is made, and is like a cake, already sliced into portions, so that the majority must stay poor because there is not enough to go around.

Because they hang on to this erroneous idea, they feel ashamed to ask for wealth, asking for just enough to make them fairly comfortable.

Wattles tells a tale of how one of his students was told to get a clear picture of the things he wanted in his mind, so that the creative thought of them could be impressed on the Formless Stuff. He was a very poor man, living in a rented house, and having only what he earned from day to day. He could not grasp the fact that all wealth was his.

So, after thinking the matter over, he decided that he might reasonably ask for a new rug and a stove to heat the house during the winter. Following the instructions given in Wattle's book, he obtained these things in a few months. Then it dawned on him that he'd not asked for enough. He went through the house he lived in, planning

The Future Is Already Moving

Somewhere right now, someone is imagining, designing, or building the thing you'll one day need.

Your role is to create the means to reward them, and everyone who helps bring it to you, when your lives intersect.

Maybe a factory worker is assembling the car you'll buy second-hand, five years from now.

You'll never meet them, but your lives will cross – in a showroom, on a driveway, on a day you can't yet see.

The car is already in motion. Focus on becoming ready to receive it.

You're Here to Build

The Universe is not finished, it is still unfolding.

When something grows scarce, new materials and technologies emerge to take its place.

There is more than enough to go around. You are not asked to live in poverty or self-denial.

You are here to contribute – to build your part of the Universe, to advance Nature, and to leave a legacy.

Ask for everything you need to fully express your creative life.

That's not greed – that's participation.

all the improvements he'd like to make in it, mentally adding a bay window here and a room there, until it was complete in his mind as his ideal home, then he planned its furnishings.

Holding and sustaining the whole image in his mind, he began living in the Certain Way, and moving toward what he wanted. Eventually, he owned the house and improved it to reflect his mental image. Then, with more determined certainty, he went on to get greater things.

It came to him – as it will come to you, if you walk the Certain Way.

Here is a reminder of the core principles:

- **There is a formless stuff from which all things are made. In its original state, it fills, permeates, and surrounds all things – even the spaces between them.**

- **A thought, held clearly and impressed into this substance, begins to shape itself into form.**

- **Nature is the living intelligence that receives and responds to thought. When we think of and sustain a clear image – with purpose and certainty – we set that image into motion, and the thing we think about begins to take shape.**

Chapter Seven
Gratitude.

The examples in the last chapter show that the first step toward getting rich is to clearly hold and direct your desire toward Nature and the formless, creative substance from which all things arise.

This is true, and you will see that in order to do so you need to relate yourself to Nature in a harmonious way.

Securing this relationship is a matter of primary and vital importance. Let's take a look at how to bring you into perfect unity of mind with Nature.

The whole process of mental adjustment and alignment can be summed up in one word – Gratitude.

First, you willingly accept that Nature is the intelligent field from which all things proceed. Second, you willingly accept that it gives you everything you desire. Third, you relate yourself to it by a feeling of deep and profound gratitude.

Gratitude

Gratitude is the key emotion that keeps you on the path.

When everything feels against you, it can be hard to feel thankful. But pausing to notice where you are and what you have – however little – lifts your mood and gives you a new perspective to face passing difficulties.

If you think you have nothing, think again. You have yourself, and your determination to change your life.

And if you lift your eyes just a little, you'll see the love of friends, the kindness of strangers, and the beauty of nature all around you. They belong to you too – and they are precious.

Say It Like You Mean It

You were probably taught to say please and thank you – but were you ever taught to feel those words?

Gratitude isn't just a habit of manners. It's a felt response – a quiet rising of the heart.

When you say "thank you," mean it. Look up. Make eye contact. Smile, even if only inwardly. Let the moment register.

The same goes for giving thanks to Nature. Don't just say it. Feel it.

You might be surprised by what happens when you do.

Many people who order their lives rightly in all other ways are kept in poverty by their lack of gratitude. Having received one gift, they cut the wires that connect them with the giver of the gift, by failing to make acknowledgment.

It's easy to understand that the nearer we live to the source of wealth, the more wealth we shall receive, and that the person who is always grateful lives in closer touch with Nature, the giver and provider, than the one who never looks to it in thankful acknowledgment.

The more gratefully we fix our minds on Nature – the source – when good things come to us, the more good things we will receive, and the more rapidly they will come, and the reason simply is that the mental attitude of gratitude draws the mind closer in touch with the source from where the gifts come.

If it's a new thought to you that gratitude brings your whole mind into closer harmony with the creative energies of Nature, think about it, and you will see that it is true. The good things you have already came to you by following certain laws. Gratitude will lead your mind out along the ways by which things come and it will keep you in close harmony with creative thought and prevent you from falling into competitive thought.

Gratitude alone can keep you looking toward Nature, the source of everything, and prevent you from falling into the error of thinking of the supply as limited – to do that collapses all you have built in your mind and intention, bringing you back to the start of your journey.

Gratitude acts like a principle of flow. If you want results, practise it not as a ritual, but as active recognition of what's already forming in the Formless Stuff and moving toward you.

The flow of gratitude is the natural principle that action and reaction are always equal, and in opposite directions.

Gratitude isn't passive – it's a creative act. When you express it to Nature, you send a signal. The response has already begun.

Thought and Formless Stuff become entangled and new shapes, ideas, and forms begin to take shape.

If your gratitude is strong and constant, the reaction in Formless Stuff will be strong and continuous – the movement of the things you want will be always toward you. You cannot exercise much power without gratitude, for it is gratitude that keeps you connected with Power.

But the value of gratitude is not just about getting stuff in the future. Without gratitude, you won't hold steady for long before dissatisfied thoughts arise.

You begin to lose ground the moment you allow your mind to dwell on things as they are, with dissatisfaction. That fixes your attention on the average, the ordinary, the poor, the squalid and mean and your mind will take the form of these things. Then you'll transmit these forms or mental images to the Formless, and the average, the poor, the squalid, and mean will come to you.

Allowing your mind to dwell upon the second-rate is to become second-rate and to surround yourself with second-rate things.

On the other hand, to fix your attention on the best is to surround yourself with the best, and to become the best.

The creative power within turns us into the image that we give our attention to.

We too are made from Formless Stuff which always takes the form of the image that is thought about.

The grateful mind is constantly fixed upon the best, therefore it tends to become the best – it takes the form or character of the best, and will receive the best.

Gratitude feeds certainty. A grateful mind expects good things, and that expectation strengthens your belief in the creative process. Every time you consciously return to gratitude, you reinforce your certainty. Without it, certainty fades – and without that inner certainty, the creative method won't work. You'll see why in the chapters ahead.

It's necessary, then, to cultivate the habit of being grateful for every good thing that comes to you and to give thanks continuously.

A Thank You To The World.

It may help to think like the animists – people who believe there are spirits in all things.

We are all made of the same stuff, so it should be easy to give thanks to your chair for standing firm under your weight and supporting you daily.

The same goes for your computer, tablet, or phone, and the apps you rely on too. Thank them for their service, and be grateful for how they help you in your work and life.

Gratitude is an energy you can extend in all directions.

People have always known this as they have said Grace, in thanks for the food they have eaten.

The Power of Attention

If you feed on negativity, you'll become filled with it – and that shuts down the flow of gratitude.

Stop the flow of negativity first, so gratitude has space to move.

Attention is creative fuel. What you look at, you begin to mirror.

In Wattles' time, attention was inward and deliberate.

Today, attention is a commodity, sliced, packaged, and sold by platforms that are designed to keep you scrolling.

But attention is still yours to give. And how you give it matters.

You can give it passively – like a robot, locked to the feed. Or you can give it intentionally – as a gift, in gratitude, toward what you wish to bring into form.

Choose carefully.

And because all things have contributed to your advancement, you should include all things in your gratitude.

Don't waste time thinking or talking about the shortcomings or wrong actions of oligarchs or billionaires. Their organization of the world has made opportunity for you – everything you receive comes to you, in part, because of them and their organisation of the physical world.

Don't rage against politicians – if it were not for them we would fall into anarchy, and your opportunities would be greatly lessened. Not all politicians are corrupt. Most enter the field of politics with the intention of changing the world for the better.

Nature has worked a long time and very patiently to bring us up to where we are in commerce and government, and it's going right on with its work. Oligarchs, politicians, and captains of industry, will become redundant as soon as they have done their work, but in the meantime they are bringing about big changes in the world.

Remember that they are all helping to arrange the lines of transmission along which your riches will come to you, so be grateful to them all. This will bring you into harmonious relations with the good in everything, and the good in everything will move toward you.

Chapter Eight
Thinking in the Certain Way

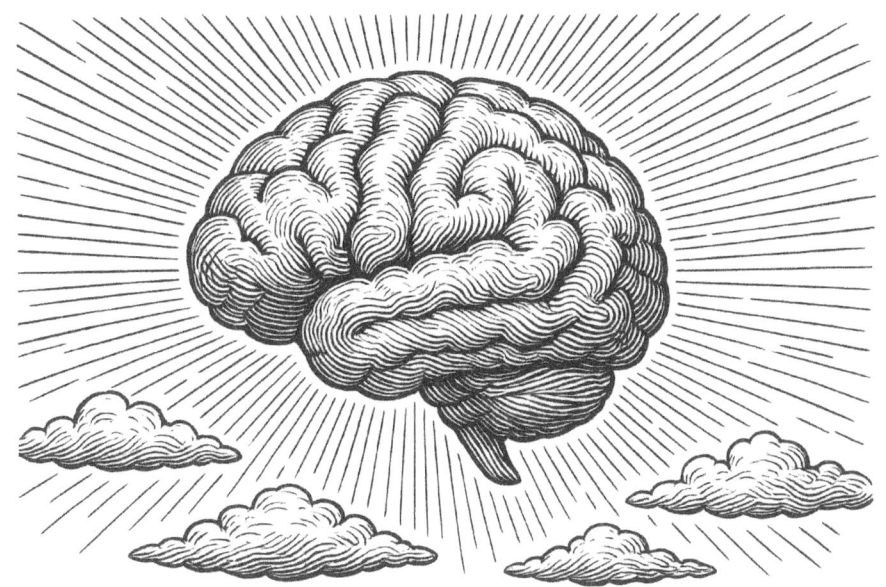

Remember the story in chapter six, of the man who formed a mental image of his house, and you will get a fair idea of the initial step toward getting rich. You must form a clear and definite mental picture of what you want. You cannot transmit an idea unless you have it yourself.

You must have the idea before you can give it. Many people fail to impress their thoughts on Nature because they have only a vague and misty concept of the things they want to do, to have, or to become.

It's not enough to have a general desire for wealth *"to do good with."* Everybody wants that.

It's not enough to just wish to travel, to see things, to live more, etc. Everybody has those desires too. If you were going to send a message to a friend, you wouldn't send the letters of the alphabet in their order, and let them construct the message for themselves. You wouldn't take words at random from the dictionary. You would send a coherent sentence, one which meant something.

Intend don't dream

There is a difference between dreaming and intending.

Dreams are wishes based on hope. You need to build your wants and desires into a vision so strong and clear in your mind that you feel you have gained them already.

Then, in your imagination, be as grateful for the gift of your newly imagined desires as if you had gained them already.

This takes hard mental work.

Belief and Outcomes

Wallace Wattles was once a Methodist minister, which is why he often quoted the Bible. Today, that language can feel at odds with science – but look past the phrasing, and the underlying principle remains clear.

In the original chapter eight, he cited Jesus:

"Whatever you ask for in prayer, believe that you have received it, and it will be yours."

You'll find similar statements in ancient philosophy, Eastern traditions, and modern psychology. The wording changes, but the structure is the same – clear intention, sustained belief, observable result.

This isn't blind faith. It's method. The science is in the outcome.

When you try to impress your wants upon Nature, remember that it must be done with a coherent statement, you must know what you want, and be definite about it.

You can never get rich, or start the creative power into action, by sending out unformed longings and vague desires.

Go over your desires in detail, just as the man in chapter six did with his house, see just what you want and get a clear mental picture of what you want, when you get it.

You must keep that clear mental picture in mind, and keep your face turned toward it at all times. Like the ship's captain keeping a constant eye on the compass and horizon, you must not lose focus or your concentration on the vision.

You don't need special rituals, affirmations, or practices to shape your reality. You simply need to know what you want – and to hold that clarity with steady intention. What you consistently give your attention to begins to take form.

Spend as much of your leisure time as you can in contemplating your picture. No one needs to take exercises to concentrate their mind on something they really want, it's the things you don't really care about which require effort to keep your attention upon.

And unless you really want to get rich, so that the desire is strong enough to keep your thoughts aligned, like a compass drawn to true north, it will hardly be worthwhile trying to carry out the instructions given in this book.

The methods set out in this book are for people whose desire for riches is strong enough to overcome mental laziness and the love of ease, and to make them work.

The more clear and definite you make your picture and the more you dwell upon it, bringing out all its inspiring details, the stronger your desire will be. And the stronger your desire, the easier it will be to hold your mind fixed on the picture of what you want.

Something more is necessary, however, than merely to see the picture clearly. If that's all you do, you are only a dreamer, and will have little or no power to accomplish your aims.

Behind your clear vision must be the purpose to make it a reality, to bring it about in tangible expression.

And behind this purpose must be an invincible and unwavering CERTAINTY that the thing is already yours, that it's "*at hand*" and you have only to take possession of it.

Live in the new house, mentally, until it takes form around you physically, and mentally enjoy all the things you want.

See the things you want as if they were actually around you all the time. See yourself as owning and using them. Make use of them in imagination just as you will use them when they are your tangible possessions.

Be just a little obsessed with your mental picture until it's clear and distinct, and then take the *Mental Attitude of Ownership* towards everything in the picture. Take possession of it in your mind, in the certainty that it's actually yours. Hold to this mental ownership. Don't waver for an instant in your certainty that it's real.

And remember what was said previously about gratitude. Be as thankful for it all the time that it is coming to you as you expect to be when it has taken form. Gratitude for what has not yet appeared is the clearest signal that your intention is aligned, that the form of your thought is already moving toward you.

Your part in all of this is to intelligently formulate your desire for the things which make for a larger life, and to get those desires arranged into a coherent whole, and then to impress this *Whole Desire* upon Nature, which has the power and the will to bring you what you want.

You don't make this impression by repeating strings of words, you make it by holding the vision with unshakable PURPOSE to attain it, and with steadfast CERTAINTY that you *will* attain it.

You cannot impress Nature by having a special day set apart to tell it what you want, and then forget about it for the rest of the week. You cannot impress it by having a special time to go to your quiet place and meditate or visualise, if you then dismiss the matter from your mind until your "*special time*" comes round again.

Not Magic Words

It's tempting to repeat affirmations like spells – hoping your words will rise up or radiate out, nudging the Universe to act faster.

But that's not how this works.

Your role is to hold a clear vision – not to beg, chant, or pester. The moment your thought becomes certain, it begins shaping the formless into form.

Then, let go and let Nature do its part.

It's already inclined to give you what you need – not as a reward, but so you can do your work and live fully.

Faith, Imagination, and Proof

Wattles wrote in the language of faith – a kind of certainty you can't prove except by holding it. That's uncomfortable for modern minds trained in data and evidence.

Faith is a chicken-and-egg thing.

Science demands proof – faith begins with belief.

But this isn't about wishful thinking. Imagination isn't a fantasy machine – it's a tool. A functional instrument of form.

You have full permission to think clearly, boldly, and constructively. Even intangible values like love, honour, or peace must be shaped in thought before they can take hold in the formless.

They don't just appear, they emerge by design and with certainty of thought.

Speaking out loud has its effect upon yourself, in clarifying your vision and strengthening your certainty, but it's not your spoken wishes that get you what you want. In order to get rich you don't need a *"mindful hour of prayer or meditation,"* you need to hold steady to your vision, with the purpose of causing its creation into solid form, and with the certainty that you are doing so.

The whole matter rests on receiving, once you have clearly formed your vision. When you have formed your vision, you might well make an oral statement, respectfully addressing Nature and the Formless Stuff, and from that moment you must, in your mind, receive what you ask for.

Live in the new house. Wear the fine clothes. Drive the new car. Go on the journey, and confidently plan for greater journeys to come. Think and speak of all the things you have asked for in terms of actual present ownership. Imagine an environment, and a financial condition exactly as you want them, and live all the time in that imaginary environment and financial condition.

However, don't do this as a mere dreamer – hold to the CERTAINTY that the imaginary is being realised, and hold to the PURPOSE to realise it. Remember that it is certainty and purpose in the use of the imagination which make the difference between the realist and the dreamer. And having learned this fact, it's now that you must learn the proper use of the WILL.

Chapter Nine
How to Use the Will

The Will

When Wattles talks about will, he doesn't mean forcing things to happen.

He means using your mental power to hold a thought steady.

Your will is yours to control.

It's your job to stay on the Certain Way – to not get distracted by quick fixes, shiny objects, or passing beliefs.

The will is like a muscle. The more you use it, the stronger it gets.

To set about getting rich in a scientific way, don't try to apply your will power to anything outside yourself. You have no right to do so, anyway.

It's wrong to apply your will to other people to get them to do what you want. It's as flagrantly wrong to coerce someone else by mental power as it is to coerce them by physical power.

If compelling others by physical force is a crime, compelling them by mental means is also a crime.

The only justification for the use of your will is to get yourself to think and act in the Certain Way.

Using your will to try to compel others to think and act as you wish, or get what you want, is a corruption of thought, and will likely do you no good.

Right Use of Will

Your will is not for forcing others or trying to control outcomes.

Your job is to use it to stay consistent – to keep impressing your thoughts into the Formless Stuff with focus and intention.

It's about inner discipline, not outer pressure.

When you know what to think and do, then use your will to compel yourself to think and do the right things. That is the legitimate use of the will – to get yourself to think and act in the Certain Way.

Don't try to project your will, or your thoughts, or your mind out into space, to act on things or people. Keep your mind within you, it can accomplish more there than elsewhere.

Use your mind to form a mental image of what you want, and to hold that vision with certainty and purpose – and use your will to keep your mind working the *right way*.

The more steady and continuous your certainty and purpose, the more rapidly you will get rich, because you will make only positive impressions upon The Formless and you will not neutralise or offset them by negative impressions.

The picture of your desires, held with certainty and purpose, is taken up by the Formless, which permeates it across great distances, bringing together the ingredients and conditions for its creation.

You don't need to do exercises in concentration, or set apart special times for meditation or affirmation, and you should not indulge in magical thinking of any kind.

All you need is to know what you want, and to want it badly enough that it will stay in your thoughts.

Spend as much of your leisure time as you can in contemplating your picture.

It's the power of desire that causes your mind to think about the picture of what you want and if you desire it so much that it is your supreme focus, you will not have difficulty holding your mind fixed on the image of your desire.

The more you dwell upon your clear and definite image, highlighting its perfect details, the stronger your desire will be – and the stronger your desire, the easier it becomes to hold your mind fixed on the image of what you want.

But something more is needed than merely seeing your image clearly. If that were all, you would only be a dreamer, and a visionary.

Bring your picture into reality by affirming that it's yours, by assuming the attitude of the person who already possesses it, by living in the present moment as if your vision were already real.

Don't sit and wait for it to come to you. Act now.

There is never any other time but now, and there never will be any other time but now. If you are ever going to get ready for the reception of what you want, you must begin now.

And the action you take, whatever it is, must most likely be in your present line of work, and must be upon the persons and things in your present environment.

You cannot act where you are not. You cannot act where you have been. And you cannot act where you are going to be – you can only act where you are.

Don't bother yourself whether yesterday's work was well done or not. Do today's work well.

Don't try to do tomorrow's work now – there will be plenty of time to do that when you get to it, tomorrow.

Don't try, by magical or mystical means, to act on people or things that are out of your reach.

Don't wait for a change of environment before you act – get a change of environment by action.

You can act in the environment where you are now, so as to cause yourself to be moved to a better environment.

Hold with certainty and purpose the vision of yourself in the better environment, but act upon your present environment with all your heart, and with all your strength, and with all your mind.

Don't spend any time in daydreaming or castle-building. Hold to the *One Vision* of what you want, and act now.

Don't Fake It – Live It

You may have heard people say, 'Fake it till you make it.' It sounds clever, but it misses the point.

This isn't about pretending or play-acting. Faking leads to internal dissonance – a split between who you are and who you're performing as. That's unsustainable.

Instead, embody the change.

Live as if your reality is already aligning. Act with clarity, walk with intention, speak with purpose.

You're not lying to yourself, you're stepping into a more accurate version of who you're becoming.

Don't fake it – be it, live it, breathe it.

45

Letting Go to Move Forward

To move ahead, you may need to leave your past behind – including places, habits, or people who are holding you back.

That might not be practical right away. So begin in your mind.

Live in the new place or situation mentally. Act in the life you're building, not from the one you're leaving behind.

If you hold the vision and play your part, the rest will start to move into place.

Chapter Ten
Further Use of the Will

You cannot retain a true and clear vision of wealth if you are constantly turning your attention to opposing ideas, thoughts and images, whether they're external or internal.

Don't speak of your past troubles of a financial nature. If you have had them – don't think of them at all.

Don't define yourself by your past – not by your parents' poverty, nor the struggles you've faced. Repeating those stories only reinforces your connection to lack.

You're not ignoring the past – you're choosing to leave it behind.

The energy you bring into the present is what shapes what comes next. If you want to move forward, you have to stop pulling the weight of what you've already left behind.

You have accepted a certain theory of Nature as being correct, and are putting all your hopes of happiness on its being correct. There is no point in flirting with conflicting theories.

Don't read, watch or listen to people that tell you that the world is coming to an end. Pay no attention to news outlets, all they want is your attention, and bad news sells best. That also goes for influencers selling you their dreams and philosophers who tell you that the world is going to the dogs.

The world is not going to the dogs – it's going to the good – it's becoming wonderful, and you are helping it to do so.

True, there may be many things that seem bad, but what is the point of analysing them when they are a passing phase, and when the analysis of them only tends to check their passing and keep them around for longer?

Why give time and attention to things that will fade in the glare of scrutiny, when you can speed their end by promoting clearer, stronger, more creative and equitable ideas?

No matter how horrible the conditions in certain countries or other places might be, you're wasting your time and spoiling your own chances by thinking about them.

You should interest yourself in the world becoming rich.

Think of the riches the world is coming into, instead of the poverty it's growing out of. And bear in mind that the only way you can help the world to grow rich is by growing rich yourself through the creative method – not the competitive one.

You don't help anyone by focusing on what's missing.

The best way to lift others is to live the example – to show what's possible through your own clarity, effort, and growth.

When people see someone moving with purpose and generosity, they don't feel judged – they feel inspired.

Stay focused on creative energy, not lack.

Let your life be proof that a better way exists.

Today Shapes Tomorrow

If you keep doing the same old thing, tomorrow will look just like today.

But the future can change in a heartbeat – the moment you snap your fingers and say, "The future starts now."

Hold your vision. Begin the work. Let a different tomorrow take shape.

Giving Is Not Self-Sacrifice

If you find yourself exhausted by constant giving – especially to people who only take – go back and re-read Chapter 5. Wattles was quite clear.

"Extreme altruism is no better or nobler than extreme selfishness – both are misguided."

The Certain Way is not about martyrdom or misery. You are not required to drain yourself to prove your worth or earn favour. Nature doesn't ask for sacrifice – it asks you to grow in a way that let's others grow too.

But just because you give your whole time and mind and thought to riches, it does not follow that you are to be selfish or mean.

To become really rich is the noblest aim you can have in life, for it includes everything else.

With a competitive mind, the struggle to get rich becomes a directionless scramble for dominance over others. But with a creative mind, everything changes.

True greatness, depth of character, meaningful service, and higher purpose all flow through the path of getting rich – not in spite of it, but through it. These things become possible through the intentional use of riches.

A person's highest happiness is found in bestowing benefits on their nearest and dearest – love finds its most natural and spontaneous expression in giving.

The person who has nothing to give can't fully play their role as a partner, citizen, or a member of society.

It's in the use of things that a person finds full life for their body, develops their mind, and unfolds their creative being. So it is supremely important that everyone should be rich.

It's perfectly okay to want to be rich. If you're a normal person, you can't help doing so.

It's perfectly right that you should give your best attention to the science of getting rich, for it's the noblest and most necessary of all studies.

If you neglect this study, you're letting yourself down, as well as humanity and Nature. You can render no greater service than to make the most of yourself.

Chapter Eleven
Acting in the Certain Way

Thought is the impelling force which causes the creative power to act. Thinking in a Certain Way will bring riches to you, but you must not rely upon thought alone, while paying no attention to how you act. That's the stumbling block. Many, otherwise thoughtful, people fail to connect thought with personal action.

We have not yet reached the stage of development, even supposing such a stage to be possible, when a person can create directly from Formless Stuff without Nature's processes or the work of human hands. A person must not only think, but their personal action must reinforce their thought.

With thought, you can draw anything you want toward you – but it won't come rolling down the road on its own, waving hello.

Under the natural order of things, someone, somewhere will have the idea to make what you want, and then find the means to create it. It may pass through many hands and countries on its way to you.

Thought Alone Won't Do It

Thought is only half the equation. The Certain Way demands action.

You won't get what you want by thinking alone.

You must move. You must work. You must put energy into your life.

Apply for the job. Start the business. Reach out. Make the offer. Look for where value is needed – and be ready to deliver it.

Don't wait for perfect conditions.

Start today.

Start now.

It's On The Way.

The new car you want might be in production – right now – in a factory on the other side of the world.

It may have to pass through a few owners and a couple of dealerships before it reaches you.

But it is already on its way. It will arrive in time. Prepare the ground. Have the money, a trade-in, credit score or something else to trade with, ready when the moment comes to receive it.

Your job is to arrange your life so you're ready to recognise and receive it when it arrives.

Your thought sets things in motion – people, materials, and events begin to align. But things don't just appear on your doorstep like an Amazon delivery .

You are not to steal them, nor to take them as charity. To receive what you desire, you must be ready to pay a fair price – and you earn that, as we've said before, by giving more in use value than you take in payment. That's how the cycle stays creative, not competitive.

The scientific use of thought means forming a clear, distinct image of what you want, holding steadily to the purpose of getting it, and realising – with grateful certainty – that it is already on its way to you.

Don't try to "project" your thought in any mystical way, with the idea of it going out and doing things for you – that is wasted effort, and will weaken your power to think with sanity.

The action of thought in getting rich is fully explained in the previous chapters. Your certainty and purpose positively impress your vision upon Formless Stuff, through Nature, which has the same desire for more life that you have, and this vision, received from you, sets all the creative forces to work in and through their regular channels of action, but directed toward you.

It's not your part to guide or supervise the creative process, all you have to do is keep to your vision, stick to your purpose, and maintain your certainty and gratitude.

But you must act in a sure and Certain Way, so that you can receive what is yours when it comes to you, so that you can meet the things you have in your mental image, and put them in their proper places as they arrive.

This is not magic. When things reach you, they will be in the hands of other people, who will ask an equivalent for them – payment or kind.

You can only get what is yours by giving the other person what is theirs, in their own mental image – money or something of equal value.

Your bank account is not going to be always full of money without effort on your part. This is the crucial point in the science of getting rich – right here, where thought and personal action must be combined.

Many people who, consciously or unconsciously, set the creative forces in action by the strength and persistence of their desires, remain poor because they don't put in place the opportunity to receive the thing they want when it comes.

By thought, the thing you want is brought to you – by action you receive it.

Whatever your action is to be, it's clear that you must act *now*. You cannot act in the past, and it's essential for the clarity of your mental vision that you clear the past from your mind. You cannot act in the future, for the future is not here yet. And you cannot tell how you will want to act in any future situation until that situation has arrived.

Just because you are not in the right line of work now, don't think that you must postpone action until the right situation comes along.

And don't waste time worrying about how you'll cope with possible future emergencies – be sure that you'll have the ability to meet any emergency when, or if, it ever arrives.

If you act in the present with your mind on the future, your present action will be with a divided mind, and will not be effective.

Put your whole mind into present action.

Don't give your creative impulse to Nature, and then sit down and wait for results. If you do, you will never get them. Act now. There is never any time but now, and there never will be. If you are ever going to begin getting ready to receive what you want, you must begin now.

And your action, whatever it is, must most likely be in your present line of work, and must involve the people and things in your present environment.

You cannot act where you are not, you cannot act where you have been, and you cannot act where you are going to be. You can act only where you are.

Don't bother about whether yesterday's work was done well or not – do today's work as well as you can.

One Thought At A Time

Cognitive dissonance is the mental strain of holding two opposing ideas at once. It creates stress, confusion, and burnout.

Clarity cuts through.

Focus on one thing. What action can you take right now that moves you toward the future you want?

Do that.

Then let the rest go.

You Make Your Luck

You don't need omens or lucky charms.

Your clarity, certainty, and decisions are what matter.

Luck is what happens when you've prepared the ground and are ready, in the right place, when opportunities arise.

Be prepared, and learn to recognise the opportunities that pass most other people by.

Don't try to do tomorrow's work now, there will be plenty of time to do that when you get to it.

Don't try, by magical, mystical or mental projection methods, to influence people or things that are out of your reach.

Don't wait for a change in your situation before you act – change your situation by action. You can work within your current situation in a way that leads you to a better one.

Hold with certainty and purpose the vision of yourself in a better place, but act where you are now with all your heart, and with all your strength, and with all your mind.

Don't waste time day-dreaming or castle building. Hold to the one vision of what you want, and act now.

Don't cast about looking for something new to do, or for some strange, unusual, or remarkable action to perform as a first step to getting rich. It's likely that your actions, at least for some time to come, will be those you've been performing for some time past, but now you must begin performing these actions in the Certain Way, that will surely make you rich.

If you're in a line of work that doesn't feel right for you, don't wait until you find the perfect job before you start taking action, there may be a job in between that is a stepping stone along the way.

Don't feel discouraged, or waste energy dwelling on the idea that you're in the wrong place currently.

No one is ever so far off track that they can't find their way to the right place, and no one is ever so deep in the wrong line of work that they can't move into one that truly fits.

Hold the vision of yourself in the kind of work you truly want, with the purpose to step into it, and the certainty that you will – and are – moving toward it. But act within your current work.

Use your present role as the path to something better, and your present surroundings as the ground where change begins.

Your vision of the right work, if held with certainty and purpose, will draw the opportunity to you, and your action, done in the Certain Way, will move you toward it.

If you are an employee and feel that you have to change jobs in order to get what you want, don't rely on thought alone to change your job. It most likely won't work.

Hold the vision of yourself in the job you want, while you **act** with certainty and purpose in the job you have, and you will get the job you want.

Your vision and certainty will set the creative force in motion to bring it toward you, and your action will cause the forces in your current situation to move you toward the place you want to be.

In closing this chapter, let's add to our statement:

- **There is a formless stuff from which all things are made.**

- **In its original state, it fills, permeates, and surrounds all things – even the spaces between them.**

- **A thought, held clearly and impressed into this substance, begins to shape itself into form.**

- **Nature is the living intelligence that receives and responds to thought. When we think of and sustain a clear image – with purpose and certainty – we set that image into motion, and the thing we think about begins to take shape.**

- **To do this, we must shift from a competitive mindset to a creative one – holding the image with fixed purpose and unwavering certainty, shutting out doubt, distraction, and fear.**

- **To receive what we desire when it comes, we must act now, within our current environment, preparing ourselves and our work to be ready.**

Be Sure. Be Certain

Certainty grows stronger with purpose when you make a decision and stick to it.

Stand tall, shoulders back.

Look confident. Feel confident.

You are moving forward in the Certain Way.

53

Don't Just Do It – Do It Right.

Nike's iconic slogan, "Just do it," works great for sport, where trained reflexes and instinct take over.

But in life and creative work, reflex alone won't cut it.

Yes – act. But act with thought, care, and precision. Do the things that move you forward.

Don't waste your time on rushed, unfocused, or unnecessary actions that drain energy and get in your way.

Effort is not the same as progress.

Chapter Twelve
Efficient Action

You must use your thought as explained in previous chapters, and start doing *all* that you can where you are right now.

You can only move forward by becoming larger than the person you are now and your place in the world at the moment. No one moves forward if they don't do the work required in their current place and situation.

You can only move forward by outgrowing who you are and where you are now. No one advances by avoiding the work at hand – growth begins with showing up fully in your present place.

The world is advanced only by those who more than fill their present places and situations.

If no one quite filled their current place, everything would start to slide backwards. No society can move forward if everyone achieves less than their potential.

Progress in life is guided by the same evolutionary logic as in the natural world. In biology, mutation and adaptation lead to evolution – not effort alone. The same is true in life – change begins with shifts in thought, that let you outgrow your current role or situation.

There never would have been new species had there not been organisms which altered and fit the new environments they found themselves in. The rules are exactly the same for you – change begins with a shift in thought that allows you to outgrow your current role and thrive in a new one that suits your skills and temperament.

New species didn't emerge by perfecting old roles, but by adapting to new conditions – or seeking out new environments altogether. The same rules apply to you – your ability to get rich depends on using this principle in your own life.

Every day is either a successful day or not. It's the successful days which get you what you want. Unsuccessful days hold you back, slow you down or bring you to a dead stop. If every day is a success, you cannot fail to get rich.

If there is something that can be done today, and you don't do it, you have failed as far as that thing is concerned. The consequences may be more negative than you can imagine or predict.

You can't foresee the results of even the most trivial action. You'll never know the workings of all the forces that have been set moving on your behalf.

A great deal may depend on your doing something simple. It might be the very thing that will open the door of opportunity that leads to the outcome you are seeking.

You can never know all the connections that Nature is making for you in the world of things and human affairs, but your neglect or failure to do some small thing may cause a long delay in getting what you want.

Do, every day, ALL that can be done that day.

There is one important exception you need to keep in mind – you are not to overwork, nor rush your new ideas in the blind effort to do the greatest possible number of things in the shortest possible time.

You've Already Said Yes.

Most people settle – not because they're lazy, but because change feels hard.

They stay where they are, telling themselves it's "good enough."

But the fact you've read this far means something else –

You've already imagined a richer, fuller life.

Now give that vision clarity. Sharpen it into something specific and certain.

Then start taking steady, creative action to bring it into being.

Marathon Mindset.

If this is all new to you, it's easy to get fired up.

You might feel ready to work through the night – and that's great.

But many people burn out fast, then slip back into old habits.

This is a long game. A marathon, not a sprint.

Be kind to yourself. Find a pace you can sustain.

Your reward is waiting at the finish line – not halfway through.

You are not to try to do tomorrow's work today, nor to do a week's work in a day.

It's not the number of things you do, but the efficiency of each separate action that counts.

Every action is either successful or it's not. Every action is either effective or inefficient. If your actions aren't effective, doing more just wastes more time. Success comes from focused, efficient effort – not from staying busy.

On the other hand, every efficient action is a success in itself, and if every action in your life is an efficient one, your whole life must be a success.

Failure comes from doing too many things in an inefficient manner, and not doing enough things in an efficient manner.

It's clear that if you don't do any inefficient actions, and do enough efficient actions, you will become rich. If you can make each action an efficient one, you can see that the getting of riches is reduced to an exact science, like mathematics.

So, everything revolves around the question of whether you can make each separate action a success in itself. And you certainly can.

You can make each action a success, because Nature is working with you, and Nature cannot fail.

Nature is at your service, and to make each action efficient you have only to put energy into it.

Every action is either strong or weak, and when every action is strong, you are acting in the Certain Way which will make you rich.

Every action can be made strong and efficient by holding your vision while you are doing it, and putting the whole power of your certainty and purpose into it.

It's here that people fail by separating their mental power from the actions they take. They use the power of their mind here, and they act over there, so their actions are unsuccessful.

But if all their energy, backed by the will of Nature, goes into every action, no matter how simple, every action will be a success.

As is the nature of things, every success opens the way to other successes, so your progress towards what you want, and the progress of what you want towards you, will become increasingly rapid.

Remember that successful action is cumulative in its results. Since the desire for more life is inherent in all things, when a person begins to move towards a larger life, more things are drawn to them, and the influence of their desire is multiplied.

Do, every day, all that you can do that day, and do each action in an efficient manner.

At the same time, hold your vision while you are doing each action, however trivial or ordinary. Focus most on the work. It's not necessary to see the vision in intricate detail, at all times.

Use your leisure hours to use your imagination on the details of your vision, and to meditate on them until they are firmly fixed upon your memory. If you want speedy results, spend practically all your spare time in this practice.

With continual thought, you will get a finely detailed picture of what you want so firmly fixed in your mind, and so completely transferred to the mind of Formless Stuff, that during working hours you need only to think of the picture to reinforce your certainty and purpose, making you want to do your best.

Contemplate your picture in your leisure hours until your consciousness is so full of it that you can grasp it instantly. You will become so enthused with its bright promises that the mere thought of it will ignite a flame within you.

Goody Bags.

At events like the Oscars, the stars walk away with goody bags full of luxury gifts. Success draws value toward it.

That's not luck – it's alignment.

When you move in sync with Nature, Nature moves in sync with you.

Keep Steady

Wattles offered short, powerful statements to anchor the mind.

Learn these by heart. Read them again when doubt or confusion creep in.

The thing you want is moving toward you, so stay certain, stay purposeful.

Don't interrupt its path with fear or hesitation.

Let us again repeat our statement:

- **There is a formless stuff from which all things are made.**

- **In its original state, it fills, permeates, and surrounds all things – even the spaces between them.**

- **A thought, held clearly and impressed into this substance, begins to shape itself into form.**

- **Nature is the living intelligence that receives and responds to thought. When we think of and sustain a clear image – with purpose and certainty – we set that image into motion, and the thing we think about begins to take shape.**

- **To do this, we must shift from a competitive mindset to a creative one – holding the image with fixed purpose and unwavering certainty, shutting out doubt, distraction, and fear.**

- **To receive what we desire when it comes, we must act now, within our current environment, preparing ourselves and our work to be ready.**

Chapter Thirteen
Getting Into the Right Work for You

Not A Weed – The Wrong Garden.

A weed is simply a plant in the wrong place.

It might be strong, resilient, even beautiful – but if it doesn't fit the gardener's plan, it gets pulled.

To thrive, it needs the right soil, the right role, the right environment.

You're no different. You might have talent, drive, and vision, but if you're planted in the wrong setting, you'll always feel out of place.

Find the environment where your nature is seen, welcomed, and valued. That's where you'll flourish.

Success, in any particular line of work, depends on you having the well-developed abilities needed to prosper.

Without musical abilities you won't succeed as a musician or teacher of music. Without practical or technical skills you can't hope to do well in building or engineering. Without tact and commercial flair you can't expect to do well in business, sales or personal services.

However, having the well-developed skills and abilities required in your particular vocation does not insure you getting rich. There are musicians who have remarkable talent, but who remain poor. There are talented builders and engineers who don't get rich. Some sales staff are great at dealing with people, but they rarely close the deal.

These different skills and abilities are tools. It's essential to have good tools, but the tools must be used in the right way.

The Physics Of Potential.

In science, potential is stored energy – ready, but not yet active.

A battery holds it. So does a seed, or a rock poised on a slope.

All it takes is a spark, the right conditions, or a small push to release it.

It's the same with you. Your potential lives in your skills, habits, desires, and thoughts.

But potential stays dormant until you focus it with intention – and release it through action.

That's how thought becomes form.

One person can take a set of tools and build a beautiful piece of furniture. Someone else can take the same tools and try to do the same, but will make a complete mess of the job. They don't know how to use good tools in a successful way.

The various abilities of your mind are the tools with which you must do the work that will make you rich. It will be easier to succeed in a line of work for which your mental tool kit is best equipped.

Generally speaking, you'll do best doing work that uses your strongest skills and abilities – the ones that come naturally to you. But that doesn't mean you're locked into one path. Don't think your vocation is irrevocably fixed by the abilities and talents you were born with.

You can get rich in any line of work. If you don't have the skills for it, you can develop them. You'll just have to sharpen your skills as you go along, instead of restricting yourself to the innate talents and abilities you were born with.

It'll be easier for you to succeed doing something you already have the well developed skills for, but you can succeed in any line of work. Any rudimentary skill can be developed, and there are few skills that can't be developed with practice and application.

You'll get rich most easily if you do what you are best suited for, but you'll get rich with most satisfaction, if you do what you *want* to do.

Doing what you want to do is life. There is no satisfaction to be had if you have to do forever, something you don't like doing, and are never able or allowed to do what you do want to do.

It's certain that you can do what you want to do – the desire to do it is proof that you have within you the power to do it.

Desire is a signal of potential.

The desire to play music is the signal seeking expression and development, that you have the potential to play music. The desire to invent something is the signal seeking expression and development, that you have the potential to create that thing.

Where there is no potential, developed or not, there is no desire. Where there is a strong desire to do something, it's certain proof that the potential to do it is strong, only needing to be developed and applied in the right way.

All things being equal, it's best to choose the line of work you have the best developed skills and abilities for. But if you have a strong desire to go into any particular line of work, you should choose that work as the ultimate end at which you aim.

You can do what you want to do, and it's your right and privilege to follow the vocation or choose the work that will be most enjoyable and satisfying.

You are not obliged to do what you don't like doing, and you shouldn't do it except as a means to an end – moving you forward to do the things you do want to do.

If you've made mistakes in the past that have put you in an undesirable line of work or environment, you may have to do what you don't like for a while yet, but you can make the doing of it happier by knowing that doing it is making it possible for you to move forward and do what you *do* want to do.

If you feel you're in the wrong line of work, don't be too quick to change direction. The best way, generally, to change your line of work or environment is by growth.

Don't be afraid to make a sudden and radical change if the opportunity is presented and you feel, after careful consideration, that it's the right opportunity – but never take sudden or radical action when you are in doubt about the wisdom of doing so.

There is never any hurry using the creative mind and there is no lack of opportunity.

When you get away from the competitive mindset you'll understand that you never need to act in haste. No one else is going to beat you to the thing you want to do – there is enough for all. If one place is taken, another and a better one will be opened for you a little farther on – there is plenty of time.

When in doubt, wait. Return to the contemplation of your vision, and increase your certainty and purpose, and always, in times of doubt and indecision, cultivate gratitude.

Desire Reveals Potential.

If you feel a strong desire to do something, it's a signal – you have the potential to do it.

Hold the image in your mind. Immerse yourself in the subject.

Ideas will begin to flow, and when they do, be ready to act, refine, and grow.

Inspiration Is Not Urgency.

A burst of inspiration can feel electric – like you need to act right now.

But rushing risks burnout, wrong turns, or collapsing the idea before it's fully formed.

Let it breathe. Let it settle. But start now. Research. Make notes. Make plans.

Dig the foundations. Make sure you are building on solid ground.

A day or two spent contemplating the vision of what you want, and in earnest gratitude that you are getting it, will bring your mind into such close relationship with Nature that you will not make mistakes when you do act.

You can come into close unity with Nature through certainty of purpose and the will to advance in life, if you have deep gratitude.

Mistakes come from acting hastily, or from acting in fear or doubt, or in forgetfulness of the right motive, which is more life to all, and less to none.

As you go on in the Certain Way, opportunities will come to you in increasing number. You will need to be very steady in your certainty and purpose, and keep in close touch with Nature, while maintaining sincere gratitude.

Do all you can do in a perfect manner every day, but do it without haste, worry, or fear. Go as fast as you can, but never hurry.

Remember – the moment you begin to hurry, you cease to be a creator and become a competitor and you start dropping back into the old mindset again.

Whenever you find yourself hurrying, call a halt. Fix your attention on the mental image of the thing you want, and begin to give thanks that you are getting it. The exercise of gratitude will never fail to strengthen your faith and renew your purpose.

Chapter Fourteen
The Impression of Increase.

WHETHER you change your line of work or not, your current actions must be rooted in the work and position you are currently in.

You can get to where you want to be by making constructive use of the work you are already doing, by doing your daily work in a Certain Way.

And, as far as your work involves dealing with other people, whether personally or by email or messaging in some form or other, everything you do should signal growth, value, and progress.

Growth is what everyone is looking for. It's the urge of Nature within them, seeking fuller expression.

The desire for growth is fundamental in all Nature – it's the basic impulse that drives the universe. All human activities are based on the desire for growth. People strive for more food, more clothes, better houses, more luxury, more beauty, more knowledge, more pleasure – more growth in something – more life.

Old Sayings, Real Wisdom

"A bird in the hand is worth two in the bush."

"All that glitters is not gold."

"The grass is always greener."

"Better the devil you know."

These sayings endure because they point to something true – certainty beats illusion.

Even if your current situation isn't ideal, it's where you are now, and that means it's where your power is now. Use it. Get into the habit of doing your best, even when things feel stuck.

This is training that builds the muscle of readiness, so when your moment comes, you don't hesitate.

You move. And when you do, you move with certainty.

Even A Glimmer

The Certain Way ignites a light within you – a quiet radiance that lights the path for others.

That light makes people feel more capable. More hopeful. More ready to grow. That's the real impression of increase.

Stand tall. Stand firm. Throw your shoulders back – and let that light shine.

It may start as a glimmer, but it will grow as you grow more certain.

In darkness, even a glimmer brings comfort. Even a glimmer can guide the way.

Every living thing needs continuous growth. When growth slows, potential fades and declines, the rot sets in and the end can't be far away.

Humans instinctively know this, and are forever seeking more. Only those who gain more retain any of it.

The normal desire for increased wealth is not an evil or reprehensible thing, it's simply the desire for a more abundant life – it's aspiration.

And because it's the deepest instinct of their natures, men and women are attracted to those who can give them more of the means of life.

In following the Certain Way, as described, you are getting continuous growth for yourself, and you are giving it to all those you deal with.

You are a creative centre, from which an impression of growth is given off to all.

Be certain of this, and let everyone you come in contact with know it is so. No matter how small the transaction – whether it's money, advice, a favour, or even the selling of a chocolate bar to a child – put into the transaction the thought of growth and mutual increase.

Give the impression of growth in everything you do, so that everyone knows that you are an **advancing person**, and that everyone gains by dealing with you. Even the people you meet in a social way, without any thought of business, without trying to sell them anything – give them the thought of growth.

You can do this by holding the unshakable certainty that you, yourself, are in the **way of growth**, and by letting your certainty inspire, fill, and permeate every action.

Do everything that you do in the firm conviction that you are a person who brings energy and direction with clarity and purpose, creating movement in others – a signal of growth they can follow.

Feel that you are getting rich, and that in doing so, you are making others rich, and sharing the benefits with all.

Don't boast or brag about your success, or talk about it unnecessarily – certainty is never boastful.

Whenever you find someone boasting, you'll find they are secretly doubtful and afraid. Simply feel sure that you are doing things the Certain Way, and let every act and tone and look express the quiet assurance that you are getting rich, that you are already rich.

Words will not be necessary to communicate this feeling to others – they will feel the sense of growth and potential just by being in your presence, and will be attracted to you.

You must also let others know that by knowing you and working with you, they will move forward and grow themselves. Always give them a use value greater than the monetary value you are taking from them.

Take an honest pride in doing this, and let everybody know it, and you will have no shortage of customers, clients or followers. People go where they gain and grow, and Nature, which desires growth in all, will move people toward you.

Your work will begin to grow in ways that surprise you – not just in results, but in opportunities. You'll start seeing new connections, fresh benefits, and the possibility of moving into more aligned, fulfilling work, if that's what you choose.

But in doing all this, you must never lose sight of your vision of what you want, or your certainty and your purpose to get what you want.

Now, here is another word of caution in regard to motives.

Beware of the insidious temptation to seek power over others.

There's a dangerous thrill in having power over others, and it can be seductive.

The desire to dominate for personal gain has caused extraordinary harm, from ancient wars to modern business empires built on exploitation.

But this drive for mastery is not the path to real wealth. It belongs to the competitive mind – the one that believes in scarcity, struggle, and hierarchy.

The Pie Is Not the Limit

It goes without saying – think creatively, not with a mindset of lack.

There isn't just one pie to be divided – your thoughts are the ingredients that create limitless pies to be shared.

This isn't about fighting for your share of what exists. It's about creating more to share with everyone.

The Golden Rule

Versions of the Golden Rule have existed across cultures long before it was popularised in the Christian tradition:

"Do unto others as you would have them do unto you."

It's not about being nice – it's about alignment.

If your vision of success wouldn't feel right on someone else, it's probably coming from competition, not creation.

The Certain Way means building a life you'd be proud and pleased to see others build too.

The creative mind works differently. It moves from a place of shared benefit. It builds, rather than conquers. It grows, and lets others grow too.

You don't need to rule over anyone to shape your environment or direct your future. In fact, the moment you start grasping for dominance, you lose your creative flow and put your progress back in the hands of chance.

The Golden Rule is a good test. Ask, "Would I want this opportunity, outcome, or advantage for others too?"

If yes – you're still walking The Certain Way.

Chapter Fifteen
The Emerging Self

The principles in the last chapter apply as much to people in professional roles and wage-earning jobs as they do to the self-employed and those in business.

Whether you're a doctor, teacher, or spiritual leader, if you can give others a real sense of growth and help them feel more alive, they will be drawn to you. You will prosper.

The health practitioner who holds a clear vision of themselves as a gifted and successful healer – and who acts every day with purpose and certainty in that vision – will find themselves in deep alignment with Nature. That kind of presence can't help but attract loyal and thankful clients and patients.

People are hungry for direction – not more noise, but grounded, creative clarity. If you've learned how to live with purpose, build real relationships, stay healthy, grow your work, and support others in doing the same, then you're already leading by example.

The Root of All Evil?

*The original phrase comes from the Bible, "**The love of** money is the root of all evil."*

But somewhere along the line, we dropped the first part – and blamed money itself.

Money isn't evil. It's a tool. A form. A symbol of exchange.

Before coins, it was cattle, salt, grain, labour, trust.

Money was invented to make trade easier – not to corrupt the soul.

The real danger isn't money. It's the worship of money – when money becomes the goal instead of the means.

That's when people lie, cheat, steal, and forget what matters.

In the Certain Way, money is fuel – not the fire.

Use it well, and it multiplies value for you and others.

Use it badly, and it burns everything down.

Lead by Resonance, Not Reach

It's easy to drift from service into performance – to start thinking that visibility, followers, or admiration are the goal.

But leadership in the Certain Way isn't about spotlight or scale.

It's about alignment.

You're not here to collect followers. You're here to grow – and walk alongside those ready to grow too.

People respond to clarity, integrity, and lived truth. If what you offer helps them build a richer, more grounded life, they'll stay connected. That's not self-promotion. That's resonance.

Lead quietly, if that's your way.

Speak boldly, if that's your gift.

But don't chase applause. Build presence. Offer substance. Let the rest follow.

When you speak from lived experience – not hype – people recognise it. They'll want to learn from you, not because you promise results, but because you offer something real.

We don't just need people talking about these truths – we need people living them. The teacher, guide, or creator who radiates health, joy, success, and love becomes living proof of what's possible. That's who people trust. That's who they'll choose to follow.

A teacher who can spark a sense of growth and purpose in their students will succeed. And any teacher who holds the certainty and purpose of advancement in their own heart will pass it on. It can't help but overflow.

The same applies to lawyers, dentists, real estate agents, insurance professionals, technicians, builders – anyone in any line of work. This way of living works for everybody.

The combination of mindset and action described in this book is unfailing. Anyone who follows it persistently and faithfully will succeed. Becoming rich is not about luck – it's about science and certainty.

This includes anyone working for a salary or hourly rate. If your job feels limiting – low pay, no room to grow – don't get disheartened. Start with your vision. Get clear, stay steady, and act with purpose.

Do every task you're given to the best of your ability – not out of hope that someone notices, but because you've decided to bring the power of success into everything you touch. Let every action, no matter how small, express your intention to grow and prosper.

But don't confuse this with trying to impress your boss. Your goal is not to please others into promoting you – because often, if you're doing your job too well, it's in their interest to keep you where you are.

Being excellent at what you do is not enough. You must also grow beyond your role.

The person who advances is the one who has outgrown their current place and knows it – who sees clearly what's next, believes in their own potential, and is committed to stepping into it.

Work with this attitude every day. Carry it before and after your shift. Make it visible in your energy, your language, your choices, so that everyone who interacts with you, from colleagues to friends, feels the pull of your upward movement. People will be drawn to it. If you can't move forward where you are, another opportunity will soon reveal itself.

There is an energy that never fails to present new opportunities to those who walk the Certain Way.

If you act with vision, certainty, and purpose, Life must support you, because in doing so, it supports itself.

There is nothing in your situation or in the wider economy that can truly hold you back. If you can't thrive in your current job, you can thrive somewhere else. When you align with the Certain Way, you'll find yourself stepping out of whatever feels limiting, and into something that fits your feeling of growth.

Once you begin this way of living, your awareness sharpens. You'll see opportunities others miss – and you'll be ready to act.

And you won't be alone. The creative intelligence of Nature will work through you and with you, bringing the right opportunities at the right time.

Don't wait for the perfect opportunity to become everything you want to be. The moment you feel drawn toward any opportunity that feels like progress – take it. It will lead you to the next step.

There is no such thing as a world without opportunities for someone living the advancing life.

It's built into the very structure of the universe that everything will support those who are growing with intention. If you act and think in the Certain Way, you will get rich.

So – to all who work for a living, in whatever form that takes – study this book with care. If you've read this far, you already know it's time. Whatever your background, this way is open to you. Step forward with confidence, and begin. This method does not fail.

The Crab Bucket

At the seaside, children catch crabs and drop them into a bucket If one tries to climb out, the others pull it back down.

Some people do the same.

When they see you reaching for something new, they'll try to keep you at their level – not out of malice, but out of fear, jealousy, or discomfort.

They see your effort, and it reminds them of what they haven't done.

That's their problem, not yours. Hold your vision. Keep climbing.

And if you want to help, don't argue – just show them what's possible – by example, not explanation.

Crashes A Certainty

Every time the stock market crashes and panic sets in, there are always a few who remain calm.

They've planned ahead, kept funds aside, and wait patiently for the right moment.

When others are selling in fear, they buy with certainty.

Why? Because they see the market not as a limited pie, but as a system that moves in cycles.

Scarcity thinking causes the crash.

Certainty, patience, and a steady plan bring the recovery – and the reward.

Chapter Sixteen
Some Cautions And Concluding Observations

MANY people will dismiss the idea that there is a science – a Certain Way – of getting rich. They hold fast to the belief that wealth is limited, and that the whole system must be changed before everyone has a chance. But that isn't how change happens.

It's not about waiting for the world to shift before you move. It's about shifting yourself – and letting that change ripple outward.

If you begin to think and act in the Certain Way, things start to move around you. Structures adjust. Opportunities emerge. The environment begins to respond.

This doesn't require approval or ideal conditions. Wherever you are, whatever your circumstances, you can step into the creative field and begin to rise. And as you do, the path will become clearer for others.

Wealth built through competition narrows the path for everyone else. Wealth built through creation widens it.

The more who succeed through creative means, the better for all. That's how change really happens – not through blame, but through example.

But remember that your thought must be always be held in a creative mindset. You must never for a moment, be drawn into thinking that the supply is limited, or into acting on the moral level of competition.

Should you fall into these old ways of thought, correct yourself instantly, for when you are in the competitive mindset, you lose the co-operation of the mind of Nature itself.

Don't spend time planning how you might meet possible emergencies in the future, but do take sensible precautions – insurance, savings, contingencies – then get back to building. Certainty doesn't mean recklessness, it means acting today with clarity, not anxiety.

Don't worry about how you will surmount obstacles that may or may not appear, unless you can plainly see that your course must be altered today in order to avoid them.

No matter how huge an obstruction may appear at a distance you will find that, if you go on in the Certain Way, it will fade away as you approach it, or that a way over, through, or around it will appear.

No possible combination of circumstances can defeat a person who is proceeding to get rich along strictly scientific lines. No one who follows the Certain Way can fail to get rich, any more than one can multiply two by two and fail to get four.

Don't waste time and effort worrying about possible disasters, obstacles, panics, or possible bad outcomes, meet such things when they present themselves to you in the moment they arrive, and you'll find that every difficulty carries with it a plan to overcome it.

Guard your speech. Never speak of yourself, your affairs, or of anything else in a discouraged or discouraging way.

Never admit the possibility of failure, or speak in a way that suggests failure as a possibility.

The Certain Way To Play

There was a child who learned Monopoly from an older brother who cheated at everything – fast-talking, bluffing, grabbing. Winning seemed to mean overpowering others. But somehow they kept on losing.

Years later, they learned the game was actually designed to teach capitalism and something else – patient strategy, slow growth, steady returns.

They tried again – no tricks, just clarity and focus. This time, they won.

That's when they realised that in games, as in life, the competitive mind scrambles. The creative mind builds.

The Detour Might Be The Path

You might have a plan that feels clear and inspired, but for some reason, it just won't take off. It fails in ways you can't explain.

Don't panic. Don't give up. Stay steady. Stay certain. Stay grateful.

Often, what feels like a setback is just life clearing the path for something better – something you couldn't yet see.

You don't need to believe in fate or destiny. Just understand that your vision is limited. Keep your focus, stay in motion, and trust that what's truly aligned will rise to meet you – often after the first plan falls apart.

Never speak of the times as being hard, or of conditions as being difficult. Times may be hard and your line of work doubtful for those who are of the competitive mind, but they won't be for you – you can create what you want, and you are above fear.

When others are having hard times and difficulty at work, you will find your greatest opportunities.

Train yourself to see the world as something still in progress – growing, evolving, not yet complete. What looks wrong or broken is often just something unfinished or not yet developed. Speak in terms of growth. Speaking otherwise chips away at your certainty – and certainty is what keeps you moving.

Never allow yourself to feel disappointed. You might expect to get or achieve something by a certain time, and not get it. This will most likely appear to be a failure to you.

But if you hold to certainty you'll find that the failure is only apparent.

Go on in the certain way, and if you don't get what you wanted, you will get something so much better that you'll see that the apparent failure was really a great success.

That is the way every seeming failure will work out for you – be certain and hold to your purpose, have gratitude, and do, every day, all that can be done that day, doing each separate act in a successful manner.

If something doesn't work out, it's because you've not asked for enough. Keep on, and a larger thing than you were seeking will come to you. Remember this.

You'll not fail because you lack the necessary talent to do what you want to do. If you go on as directed, you will develop all the talents you need to do the work.

It's not for this book to deal with the science of cultivating talent, but it's as certain and simple as the process of getting rich.

However, don't hesitate or waver or fear that when you come to any new situation or difficult place that you will fail for lack of ability.

Keep right on, and when that moment arrives, the ability will come to you. The same source of ability that has enabled the towering heroes and heroines of history to do their greatest work is open to you You can draw upon the same source for wisdom to use in meeting the responsibilities which are laid upon you. Go on sure of yourself in the Certain way.

Study this book. Make it your constant companion until you have mastered all the ideas contained in it. While you're grounding these ideas in your mind, it helps to step back from distractions – especially the endless scroll of opinions, rabbit holes, conspiracies, propaganda and persuasive voices online.

Give yourself time and space to let these concepts settle.

Avoid environments – physical or digital – that pull your focus in conflicting directions.

You're not shutting the world out. You're tuning yourself into a new and wonderful idea.

When It Seems Not to Work

At some point, almost everyone hits the wall. Things stall, slip, or seem to fall apart. The results don't arrive. The momentum fades. Doubt creeps in – not just in the method, but in yourself.

It's tempting, in that moment, to blame the teaching. Or to double back and blame yourself. Most people do one or the other. But neither response helps.

The truth is simple – if you stop doing the work, the work stops working.

This isn't punishment. It's just the structure of things. You don't get fit by exercising once, or become a musician by thinking about practice. Form comes from effort. Effort comes from thought. Thought comes from certainty. Break the chain, and the form dissolves. That's not failure – it's the science.

So when someone says, "This doesn't work", they're usually speaking from a fracture – a break in consistency, clarity, or commitment. And

The Economy of Attention

In the online world, you're not just scrolling – you're being sold.

Your attention is the product. Every click, every swipe, every second you watch is tracked, packaged, and sold to advertisers.

These systems aren't neutral. They're designed to keep you distracted, reactive, and uncertain – because uncertainty holds attention longer.

But certainty is your edge. The more focused and intentional your thinking, the less influence these systems have over you.

Reclaim your attention. Direct it like a spotlight. Put it on what matters – your vision, your purpose, your next action. That's how you stay in the creative mindset.

The Illusion of Wealth

It's easy to be impressed by the appearance of wealth – big cars, big houses, big claims. But many of those lives are built on debt, not riches – mortgages, credit agreements, and bills you never get to see.

Real wealth is often quiet.

Truly wealthy people don't need to prove anything – they drive sensible cars and live in comfortable, lived-in homes. The substance is there, even if the surface doesn't shout.

when a teacher says, "You just didn't believe hard enough," they're often protecting their method instead of examining the structure.

Both are missing the point.

This process isn't mystical. It's real. And because it's real, it obeys laws – like gravity or growth. If you drop the work, the growth slows. If you keep digging up the seed to see how it's doing, the seed can't root. If you scatter your energy across ten projects, none get the depth to emerge.

That's not on you. That's not on the book or the idea. That's just how form works.

There's another illusion that trips people up – luck.

People love to chalk success up to luck – or lack of it. But luck, in Wattles' terms, is simply alignment plus readiness. You keep showing up. You do the work. You walk the path. And one day, what seemed like chance is revealed as the inevitable meeting of preparation and opportunity.

You make your own luck by being in the right place at the right time. And you'll be in the right place by moving in the right direction.

There will be slow days. Doubt days. Days when nothing seems to move. That's when most people drop off – not in protest, but in drift. They get distracted. They look for quicker fixes. They become unsure, uncertain.

But those who keep on – who keep doing the work, keep thinking in a Certain Way – are the ones who see results. Because this isn't a reward system like some suggest. It's not a catalogue to choose from and wait for delivery. It's not personal. It's structural.

Nature, the Thinking Stuff, responds to consistent, coherent intention. If it seems not to work, it's usually because the certainty was lost or because a different plan and opportunity are unfolding – not because Nature failed.

There's a saying, "God helps those who help themselves." But you don't need theology to understand the truth behind it.

Movement creates momentum. Form responds to direction. Nature meets us halfway – but only once we've taken the first step.

Don't sit still and wait for life to improve, begin. Move. Signal readiness through action. And as you do, opportunities, resources, and people will begin to align. It's not divine favour. It's natural law.

When you help yourself – by thinking clearly and acting with purpose – help has a place to land.

Don't read pessimistic or conflicting literature, or get into arguments about what you have learned. Do very little reading outside the ideas in this book, and be careful of watching the news. Stay up to date by all means but remember that they are not bringing you news, but stories to grab your attention – and bad news attracts attention most. Your attention is the product they sell on to advertisers.

Spend most of your leisure time contemplating your vision, cultivating gratitude, and reading this book. It contains all you need to know of the science of getting rich and you will find all the essentials summed up in the following chapter.

The final thought

Hold the thought. Do the work. Stay the course. Stay Certain.

If you can do that – not once, but daily – the form will follow.

That's not wishful thinking. That's the Certain Way.

Chapter Seventeen
Summary of the Certain Way

There is a formless stuff from which all things are made.

In its original state, it fills, permeates, and surrounds all things – even the spaces between them.

A thought, held clearly and impressed into this substance, begins to shape itself into form.

Nature is the living intelligence that receives and responds to thought. When we think of and sustain a clear image – with purpose and certainty – we set that image into motion, and the thing we think about begins to take shape.

To do this, we must shift from a competitive mindset to a creative one – holding the image with fixed purpose and unwavering certainty, shutting out doubt, distraction, and fear.

To receive what we desire when it comes, we must act now, within our current environment, preparing ourselves and our work to be ready.

You can get in tune with Nature by keeping a lively and sincere gratitude for the benefits it bestows upon you. Gratitude will unify your mind with Nature, so that your thoughts are received by it. You can remain in a creative mindset only by uniting with Nature through a deep and continuous feeling of gratitude.

You must form a clear and definite mental image of the things you want to have, to do, or to become, and hold this mental image in your thoughts, while being deeply grateful that all your desires are granted to you.

The person who wants to get rich must spend their leisure hours contemplating their vision in the certain knowledge and gratitude that the reality is being given to them.

The importance of frequently contemplating the mental image, together with certainty and devout gratitude, cannot be stressed enough. This is the process by which the impression is given to the Formless Stuff, and how the creative forces are set in motion.

The creative energy works through the established channels of natural growth, and through the systems of business, industry and social order. Everything that's included in your mental image will come if you follow the instructions given above, and if your certainty does not waver. What people want comes through the channels of work, exchange, and shared value, through trade, employment and cooperation

In order to receive, when the time comes, you must be active, and this activity must be about more than filling your current situation. You must keep in mind the reason and purpose you want to get rich, through the realization of your mental image.

And you must do, every day, all that can be done that day, taking care to do each act in a successful manner. You must give to everyone a use value greater than the monetary value they receive, so that each transaction makes for more life to all. And hold your mindset steady on progress, so others can feel that energy radiate from you – a quiet but unmistakable sense of increase.

The men and women who practice the instructions in this book will certainly get rich, and the riches they receive will be in exact proportion to the definiteness of their vision, the certainty of their purpose and the depth of their gratitude.

Postscript

I first came across the book, The Science of Getting Rich, when I had, "a pressing need for money," as the author, Wallace Wattles puts it in his preface. I had my kids at university, credit card debt, mortgage and car repayments going out every month, and I was doing everything I could think of to keep afloat. I felt like my back was up against the wall.

The book had a profound effect on me, and my situation.

It took me a while to understand what Wattles meant by the word 'certain'. It seemed like he was talking about something mystical that would be revealed if I knew the secret, if I could find the key. But there was no secret, the answer was in the title all along – The SCIENCE of Getting Rich.

"Certain", in the language of science, means sure, following a formula, sticking to a plan. There was no mystery to it, though some of Wattles' ideas have been wrapped up in clever marketing that imply there are further secrets to be revealed in courses and master-mind groups. I'm sure that's not what Wattles intended. Science seeks clarity.

Did I get rich? Well, I'm certainly not a millionaire, but then, I didn't want to be – wealth has its drawbacks as well as its advantages. Wattles tells us that riches are a means to reach your full potential, to buy time and the things you need to follow Nature's calling – to be the complete person you can and want to be. You can spend a life signalling your wealth with yachts, fast cars, champagne and swimming pools, but that is a shallow life, not a rich one.

As my circumstances improved, I realised that Wattles was teaching me that riches are not measured in purely monetary terms – although Wattles did like to talk hard cash!

Once my life was running smoothly, I didn't forget the lessons, but I didn't apply them so rigorously, so scientifically, and my progress began to slip and even halt.

Each time this happened the book came back into my life and put me back on track. Each time I learned something new and felt I was beginning to understand this man, Wallace Wattles.

He lived at an extraordinary time, the so-called *Gilded Age,* when big business trusts – Steel, Coal, and the Railroads – dominated the economy. The owners of those companies had an out-sized influence on government and the everyday lives of people around the world. There are many echoes of that time in the age we are living through today.

As Wattles was thinking and putting his ideas together, Science was roaring ahead. He published his book between Einstein's two great theories of relativity. The foundational work that led to quantum physics, was in a ferment. It was an exciting time to live if you were interested in science – the secrets of existence were being revealed.

There isn't a lot known about Wattles. I think today he might be labelled neurodivergent. His mind worked on different levels. He seems to have been interested in everything. He held a position in the Methodist Church, but was asked to leave due to the unorthodox ideas that emerged from his studies of many different religions and philosophies. Wattles was able to see and clarify underlying patterns that connected philosophy, theology and physics.

I've always had an interest in physics and Wattles made me dig deeper into the quantum physics that he seemed to have instinctively sensed. I could see where he wanted to go, but he didn't have the language or models to help him explain his ideas in full, ideas drawn from both physics and the wisdom passed down the ages. Some ideas are timeless and consistent, being repeated again and again across the range of different philosophies and theologies.

This book came back into my life yet again just when I was ready for it. I found I was reading it with new eyes. Not as the illustrator, YouTuber or children's author that I had been working as for decades – but as someone wrestling with what it means to be creative person in a world that feels increasingly fast, fragmented, and artificial.

What drew me back in was the rigour. The simplicity. The way Wattles asks us to think, clearly and deliberately, in service of what we want to create, not in service to the systems and platforms that exploit the generous nature of creative people. Not to daydream a new life into existence, but to shape it. To collaborate with Nature. To hold a steady image of potential, then do the work to achieve it.

This is something I had almost done instinctively all my life, but had never quite followed through. Here were the missing pieces. Vision, persistence, resilience and gratitude.

I started to see links I'd missed before. Not just to philosophy, but to physics – real physics. Field theory. Observation. Wave collapse. The sense that reality is participatory. That attention isn't just passive watching, but an active force, something we give or have taken from us. Wattles didn't use that language, but he was pointing toward it. The more I understood, the more it felt like his work belonged to a conversation that science is just now catching up to.

And yet, the book's language belongs to another age. The early 1900s was a golden age of invention, electricity, emergence. Wattles' world was on fire, charged with new ideas. But the tone of the book can sound strange to modern ears – moralistic, repetitive, patriarchal. Worse, it's since been turned into a kind of mystical vending machine by people selling short-cuts.

That's not what this book is.

This isn't a how-to-get-rich-quick manual. It's a way of thinking. A discipline of thought and action that builds form over time. It's for people who want to make something real – money, a business, a book, a skill, a better life – and are willing to do the slow work of holding their vision steady, even when the world doesn't seem to reward it.

So I've re-imagined the book, not to replace Wattles, but to reflect him more clearly. I've stripped away the mysticism, softened the theology, and grounded the principles in a modern framework – one that still honours the heart of what he was saying, but with the scientific knowledge that a century of examination and exploration has revealed.

I've added sidebars where I think reflection, nuance, or a bit of honest modern context might help. There is space left for you to add your own thoughts and perceptions. You are allowed to write in the book – don't hold back, make it your own – I give you permission!

This version is for creative-minded people – not just artists and musicians, but the teachers and builders – anyone who's ever felt the push of an idea asking to be born and nurtured. It's for those who've burned out, doubted themselves, or felt out of step with the noise of the world.

Re-imagining this book is the start of a new path for me, something I've felt called to do as a thank you and a service to the memory and work of Wallace D. Wattles, and in memory to my father and grandfather. They were both seekers after truth, and I suppose I have inherited the same genes.

You can follow my progress on my website, fallowground.uk, as I delve deeper into these ideas and share my thoughts and insights through writing and videos.

The Certain Way isn't the only way through this world, but it's a way that's helped me. Thanks for walking with me this far.

– Shoo Rayner

fallowground.uk

Glossary of Terms

A guide to the language of creative practice, as used in The Certain Way

Foundational Concepts

Formless Stuff

The deep, unseen layer of potential from which all things emerge. It is slow, causal, and vast – like fertile soil waiting for seed of an idea to be dropped into it. In Wattles' terms, this is the original substance. In modern language, it parallels causal elements in the quantum field.

Thinking Stuff

Nature's active, responsive intelligence. This is not separate from Nature, but Nature's own mind – the organising field that receives thought and begins the process of shaping it into form.

Nature

Used throughout this book instead of "God" or "Universe," Nature is the creative intelligence that underlies reality. It is not mystical, but responsive, lawful, and participatory.

Form

The visible, tangible result of thought impressed into the formless stuff – whether it be an object, a project, a moment, or an outcome. Form is not static, it emerges, sustains for a time, and then dissolves.

The Creative Process

Imagination

The generative faculty through which thought is formed and placed into the formless. Imagination is not escapism, but a method of shaping intention into a clear internal image.

Certainty

The modern, secular re-framing of faith. Certainty is the consistent, steady stance that sustains the emergence of form. It does not mean ignoring doubt, but holding focus through it.

Gratitude

Not sentiment, but a relational act – a way of entangling present intention with future form. Like quantum entanglement, gratitude creates resonance between now and what is becoming.

The Cut

A layered concept describing the threshold where thought becomes form. There are multiple cuts · psychological, temporal, dimensional, and personal. The Cut is the crossing point where potential collapses into actuality.

Lattice Seeding

The moment of planting an intention into the formless layer – establishing structure for emergence.

Ripple-Forming

The visible or energetic expansion of a form from its seed-point. Ripples depend on certainty to maintain their energy – if certainty weakens, the ripple may stall or recede.

Field, Energy, and Structure

Field

The relational space in which influence operates. A field is not just physical but cognitive and social. The creative field is shaped by presence, attention, and intention.

Node

A point of energy, presence, or influence – often where forms, people, or ideas intersect. Nodes are where meaning gathers.

Difference

The seed of form. Like the mathematical output of subtraction, which is always a positive, difference creates space. Culturally, it is often punished – but in the creative process, it is essential. Without difference, nothing new can emerge.

Subliminal

Not hidden, but almost formed. A formative signal close to breaking through into awareness or structure – a potential not yet actual. If certainty fades, subliminal forms may dissolve back into the formless.

Uncertainty

Often misunderstood as weakness or doubt, uncertainty is in fact the creative tension in which form begins. It is the space before decision, the openness before focus. In quantum terms, uncertainty describes the limits of simultaneous knowledge – but in the creative process, it is the necessary condition in which potential gathers.

To hold a clear image within uncertainty is not to reject doubt, but to move forward despite it. Certainty is not the absence of uncertainty – it is the stance we take within it.

Collapse

In quantum terms, collapse is the moment when potential resolves into one actual outcome – when the wave becomes a particle. In this book, collapse represents the point at which a thought, clearly held and consistently supported by action, becomes real.

Collapse is not destruction, but actualisation. It is the moment form appears. In the creative process, collapse can be triggered by clarity, sustained certainty, and readiness – or reversed when energy fades and focus is lost.

Context and Application

Mental Health

Re-framed here as a structural resonance issue, not individual pathology. Many struggles come not from personal failure but from misalignment with systems that are out of tune with human nature – especially for creative and neurodivergent individuals.

Attention

The currency of creativity. Attention collapses possibility into form. It is either given passively (as in platform economy) or actively (as a gift). Learning to direct attention is the root of creative power.

Generative Transformer

A reclaimed term. Originally from AI, here it describes a human who takes in wide-ranging ideas, structures them, and produces new, meaningful output. Wallace D. Wattles was a generative transformer of his age. This book continues that function today.

Wallace D. Wattles

www.ingramcontent.com/pod-product-compliance
Lightning Source LLC
Chambersburg PA
CBHW060926170426
43192CB00025B/2908